THE
BEHAR
MASSACRE

The execution of 69 survivors from the

British Merchant Ship "Behar"

in 1944 by the Imperial Japanese Navy

by
David Sibley

MD/JAG/FS/JM/23

CONFIDENTIAL

Office of :-

The Judge Advocate General,
6, Spring Gardens,
Cockspur Street,
LONDON, S.W.1.

3 February, 1947.

Dear *Macleod*

Sinking of M.V. "BEHAR" and Alleged
Massacre of 69 Survivors thereof.
-=-=-=-=-=-=-=-=-=-=-=-=-=-=-=-=-

I am sorry to have to trouble you again on this
matter, but I have now received photographs which are alleged
to portray certain Japanese concerned in this incident.   I
enclose copies of these photographs and I shall be grateful
if you will study them carefully and let me know at your
earliest convenience whether you can identify the persons portrayed therein.   If you can, I shall be grateful if you will
set out in your reply what you know about the participation
of these Japanese in any ill-treatment (such as assault or
neglect) of survivors of the M.V. "BEHAR" subsequent to their
being picked up by the cruiser "TONE".   In the event of your
being able to identify and give evidence against the persons
portrayed in the photographs I will make the necessary arrangements for you to swear a further affidavit locally containing
this evidence.

I shall be very grateful if you will treat this matter
as extremely urgent as the trial of the Japanese alleged to be
concerned in the Behar Incident is due to start very shortly
and this further evidence is essential.

Please return the photographs with your reply, for
which I enclose a franked addressed envelope.

Yours

C.S.C. *(signature)*

A. Macleod, Esq.,
18, Marrybank,
Stornoway,
Isle of Lewis,
Ross & Cromarty.

/JW

Aberdeen Man Death: Japs For Trial

MR. HECTOR HUGHES, M.P. for North Aberdeen, has been informed that facts about the murder of Chief Engineer Joseph N. Craig, of Aberdeen, and other members of the crew of the British merchant ship Behar at Batavia in March, 1944, will be revealed at the war criminal trial of seven Japanese in Hong Kong next month.

Scot accuses a Jap admiral

HONGKONG, Friday.—An affidavit from Angus McLeod (18), of Stornoway, was introduced at the trial in Tokyo today of Rear-Admiral Naomasa Sakonju and Captain Haruo Mayazumi, Japanese 16th Squadron, charged with the murder of about 65 British and Australian prisoners after the sinking of the British vessel Behar in the Indian Ocean in 1944.—B.U.P.

THE BEHAR MASSACRE
by David Sibley

Published by A. Lane Publishers, 61 Charles Street,
Stockport, SK1 3JR England.

Typeset by ArtWorkShop, Stockport, SK1 3AY England.

Printed and bound by e-print Limited, Dublin, Ireland Tel: (01)8304141

ISBN 1.897666.13.6

Price £8.50

PREFACE

This is the story of a little known incident of the sea-war conducted against the Allied merchant ships during the Second World War, and yet it was far more horrific than most, and possibly the worst atrocity to befall a British merchant ship during that war. Whilst much has been written about merchant ships that became victims of German U-boats, warships and commerce raiders, or the convoys across the Atlantic, and those to Russia or Malta, very little has ever appeared concerning the "BEHAR" apart from one chapter in a book written by Captain Bernard Edwards, concerning atrocities to Merchant Seamen committed by the Japanese.

In over 30 years at sea I had never read anything concerning this vessel, or heard anyone talk about it. I only became aware in the early spring of 1995 of the bare outlines of the story, after reading the book by Captain Edwards published in 1991. I soon realised that there was a great deal more to it than the intriguing chapter in "Blood & Bushido". Why had so little been written about the "BEHAR" atrocity? I discovered that Lord Russell of Liverpool had written a few pages concerning the story in his well known book "Knights of Bushido", and that there had been a war crimes trial concerning the incident, but again it did not give the full story. Inquiries to many national newspapers concerning the trial brought little response, in fact it is true to say that most did not even bother to reply.

My next line of investigation was to try and locate records that may have existed with the ship's owners, but here again this was a failure. The "BEHAR" was owned by the Hain Steamship Co Ltd, a company that had it's origins in St. Ives Cornwall, but in 1917 was taken over by the P & O Steam Navigation Co Ltd., who allowed Hain's to operate with its own management and personnel, although by the 1960s it had become Hain-Norse Ltd., after another tramp ship company owned by P & O was merged with Hain's. However by the mid 1970s the company name disappeared, and the offices

1

closed down. Not only did the name disappear, but so did the company records, and inquiries to P & O could shed no light on what had happened to the records of the Hain Steamship Company. Certainly nothing concerning the loss of the "BEHAR" or those Officer's and men that survived the ordeal at the hands of the Japanese exists at P & O head office.

However from the General Registry of Shipping & Seamen I was able to obtain copies of the Crew List, and eventually I came into contact with the former Registrar at Cardiff, who was to set me on a course which eventually lead to the Public Records Office at Kew, where from one file led me to others which produced much documentation, but I feel it would be rash of me to state that all has been found. However the material found cannot be disputed, and most probably as near to the truth as ever will be revealed so long after the events. The files were kept secret for at least 30 years. Here then was the reason why so little has been published before concerning the incident. Apart from literally a few lines in the national press on 30th October 1947 announcing Japanese Rear-Admiral Sakonju had been sentenced to death for war crimes, concerning the killing of 65 survivors from the m.v. BEHAR nothing more was printed in the press. There were so few survivors, and of those, only two are known to be still living today in the U.K.

One point which clearly comes through reading the affidavits, is that each person's perception of what he witnessed varies in detail but not substance, on reporting the same event or events. It was surprising to discover that the different authorities dealing with the case managed to get the names of the Japanese ship, and the names of the accused incorrectly spelt quite frequently. More surprising however was the "CHARGE SHEET" against the accused Japanese of the approximate killing of 65 survivors, when the Judge Advocate's Office in February 1947 already knew the true figure to be 69, to which they referred in a letter to Mr Angus Macleod, a survivor from the "BEHAR".

2

No report of the attack on the "BEHAR" or his experiences after being captured could be found from the Master of the "BEHAR", who survived captivity. In fact all the affidavits used in the war crimes trial, came from the service personnel, signed on as "deckhands", and from three passengers. The 1st Radio Officer gave a sworn affidavit concerning ill treatment on a Japanese cargo ship taking him and five others from the "BEHAR" on a voyage from Java to Japan.

In view of the passage of time since the events of 1944, with so few European survivors, I decided that the story, all of which is verifiable, could best be told by providing a text linking many of the documents discovered. With a few minor exceptions, I have re-copied all the files as found, hence the variations of spellings referred to above.

David Sibley
East Ayton
January 1997

ACKNOWLEDGEMENTS

The author acknowledges with appreciation, the following sources of information: Public Records Office Kew, the Marine Safety Agency Registry of Shipping & Seamen Cardiff, The Guildhall Library London, The New Zealand Defence Force. To the following individuals: Gabe Thomas former registrar at the General Register of Shipping & Seaman, Charlotte Havilland of John Swire & Sons Ltd. Survivors of the "BEHAR" Mr. W.L. Griffiths and Mr C.P.H. Kershaw. Mr W.A. Phillips, son of the late Mr W.Phillips Chief Officer of the "BEHAR", Mrs Mary Macleod, Mrs Eileen Macleod who sent information relating to Mr Angus Macleod, a survivor from the "BEHAR". Captain Bernard Edwards, who so kindly allowed me access to material he held concerning the story, upon which I was able to expand in greater detail as my research uncovered material which had been kept secret for decades. I would also like to express my great gratitude to my friend and researcher Geoff Drummond, who helped me unravel the true identities of service personnel sailing on the ship as DEMS crew, but signed on as "Deckhands". The photograph of the "BEHAR" is produced by kind permission of P & O Steam Navigation Co Ltd., London.

All documents from Public Records Office are crown copyright and are reproduced with the permission of the Controller of Her Majesty's Stationery Office and full document reference is given where appropriate.

AUTHOR'S NOTE.

Various offices and administrations involved in the investigation into the war crime associated with the BEHAR" incident used different spellings for the Japanese accused in the crime, the names are shown as found in the documents. Similarly with reference to the rank held by SAKONJU Naomasa, who is variously described as a Rear Admiral and Vice Admiral.

However where the author's own text appears concerning the two accused, the spelling and rank appear as Rear Admiral Sakonju and Captain Mayazumi, which is how the two accused are described by the military authorities when releasing information to the media concerning the Military Trial. In affidavits from the Captain of the cruiser "TONE" his name appears variously as Mayuzumi and Mayazumi.

THE HAIN STEAMSHIP COMPANY. LIMITED.

a13.

TELEGRAPHIC ADDRESS:
"TRELAWNY, STOCK, LONDON."

TELEPHONE Nº
AVENUE 5901 (3 Lines)

Baltic Exchange Chambers.
St. Mary Axe, London, E.C.3.

ED/JAG/FS/JM/23(2G).

CONFIDENTIAL.

Judge Advocate General,
Spring Gardens,
Cockspur Street,
LONDON, S.W. 1.

8th March, 1947.

Dear Sir,

<u>Japanese War Crimes. Sinking of m.v. "BEHAR"</u>
<u>and Alleged Massacre of 69 Survivors thereof.</u>

We are in receipt of your letter of the 6th instant, and note you are endeavouring to discover the fate of Gordon Henry Cumming, who was listed as 3rd Radio Officer on board the above named vessel when she was sunk by the Japanese cruiser "TONI" in the Indian Ocean on the 9th March, 1944.

In reply to your enquiry, we have to advise you that the Director General, Ministry of War Transport, Berkeley Square House, London, S.W. 1., writing to us on the 13th April, 1946 under reference M.14553/45, advised that it had then been established that the survivors of the m.v. "BEHAR", who were taken aboard the Japanese cruiser which sank the vessel and who were not subsequently landed in Batavia, were executed on the cruiser on the night of the 18/19th March, 1944.

We were requested that this information should be communicated to the next of kin with an expression of the Minister's deepest sympathy. At the same time we were asked to inform the

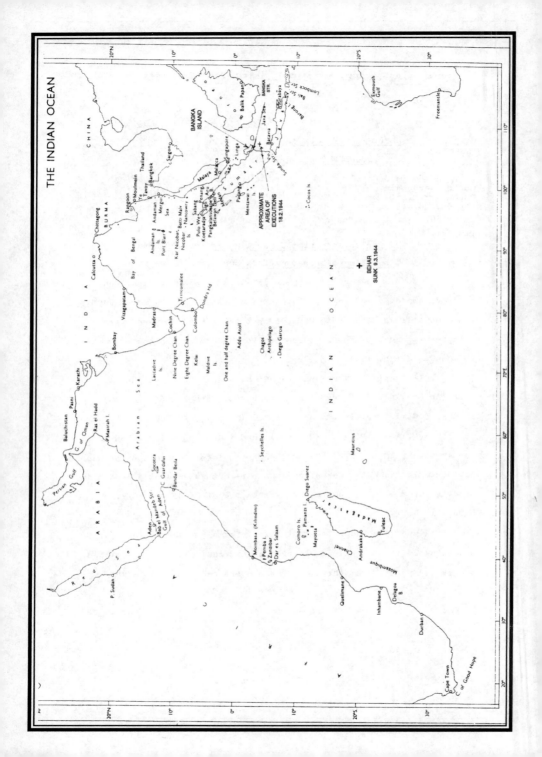

THE INDIAN OCEAN

IN MEMORY OF ALL THOSE FROM

THE M.V. BEHAR

WHO LOST THEIR LIVES

WHILST IN JAPANESE HANDS

NO ONE IS FORGOTTEN

NOTHING IS FORGOTTEN

OPERATION "SAYO No.1"

In August 1943 a fine ship was completed at the Barclay, Curle & Co. shipyard. Not the ordinary basic standard war built cargo ship type for government account, but a high class cargo liner, a vessel of 7,840 tons gross, twin screw motorship with a speed of 15½ knots. She looked every inch like a typical P & O cargo liner, but was in fact built for the Hain Steamship Co. Ltd., of London, which was a subsidiary company of the P & O Steam Navigation Company. This ship was the "BEHAR", the sister ship of the "SOCOTRA", which just a few months previously had also been completed by Barclay Curle shipyard on the Clyde, but unlike the her sister which was to last until 1965 before being scrapped in Hong Kong, her life was to last only a few short months.

The ship had a compliment of 98, comprising of 18 Officers, 61 Indian, 2 Chinese crew, and 17 DEMS personnel. The Master, 51 years old Captain Maurice Symons, was born in the West Country but living in Glasgow, the Chief Engineer, James MacKay Weir aged 58 came from Glasgow, and had stood by the ship whilst it was being built, all the remaining 7 engineers also came from Glasgow or other parts of Scotland. The Chief Officer William Phillips hailed from Cardiff, the other deck officers being the 2nd, 3rd,& 4th Officers plus 2 apprentices. The Radio Department which in peacetime would have only 1 Radio Officer, carried 3 Radio Officers, in order to maintain a continuous 24 hour radio watch, Arthur Walker being the 1st Radio Officer.

It was normal wartime practice to defensively arm merchant ships, and supply them with a "DEMS" crew to man the guns, these men came from the Royal Navy and the Army. The Royal Artillery providing a Maritime Regiment contingent. The "BEHAR" was well equipped, the defensive armament consisting of 4 inch and 3 inch dual purpose guns, Oerlikon guns, machine guns, and rocket launcher. In addition, but unusual for a merchant ship, she was fitted with ASDIC for the detection of submarines. Four Royal Navy Asdic operators were carried to operate the ASDIC set. Petty Officer W. L. Griffiths leading the "DEMS" gunners, whilst A. B. Charles Kershaw was in charge of the ASDIC team. To avoid any diplomatic embarrassment should a ship visit a neutral country, the ship could not have on board armed service personnel, so to get round this problem, the "DEMS" personnel were signed on as "deckhands". No trace of their service identities existed in the ship's articles which lists all the crew, who signed on, and in which capacity they were engaged.

After completion of shipyard trials, the "BEHAR" was handed over by the shipbuilders to the owners, and sailed from the Clyde anchorage on 21st August for Birkenhead to load cargo for India. The vessel returning to the Clyde to await an Eastbound convoy, finally leaving the anchorage on 15th September 1943 bound for Port Said. After calling at Aden the vessel proceeded in convoy for three days, before sailing independently for Cochin. Followed by calls at Bombay and Karachi, where at the former port, rice and cement was loaded for Calcutta. Whilst the ship was at Bombay in November 1943, the 3rd Radio Officer James Cuthbert left the ship, and was replaced by another young Radio Officer, Henry Gordon Cumming; for Cuthbert this move without doubt was to save his life.

At Calcutta the next cargo was loaded for Australia, sailing via Colombo. Following Australia the vessel sailed for New Zealand where cargo was loaded at Wellington, and five passengers joined the ship for passage to India via Australia. Three of the passengers being Royal New Zealand Navy Officers attached to Fleet Air Arm of the Royal Navy. Another passenger to join was a Royal New Zealand Air Force Flight Sergeant, whilst the last passenger a Chinese Doctor of Agriculture by the name of Lai Yung Li who was on his way to Chungking. From Wellington the vessel proceeded to Sydney, Newcastle N.S.W. and finally Melbourne, where more passengers joined. Two ladies, on their way to re-join their husbands in India, and a Mr. Duncan McGregor a retired elderly gentleman, of Scottish origin and a former bank manager in Nairobi, Kenya. He now lived in Burwood, Victoria and was on his way to Kenya via India. The last passenger to join on the 28th February 1944, being Captain Percy James Green, a Merchant Navy captain, employed by the China Navigation Company on his way to India to rejoin a company vessel, after a period of leave in Australia.

By the beginning of 1944 the tide of fortune was flowing in favour of the Allies, the Battle of the Atlantic had been won, Italy had surrendered, the Russians were pushing the invaders out of her territory, whilst the Japanese after their successful onslaught in the Far East, and Pacific Islands, had in June 1942 suffered a decisive naval defeat at Midway Island. Guadalcanal finally fell in February 1943. Later in the year, there were successes for Americans and Australians, in New Guinea. The Americans made landings in the Solomon Islands, and Gilbert Islands. The might of American naval and air power was beginning to be felt more and more by the Japanese in the Pacific regions. However the Japanese were very firmly in control in the mainland Far East and Dutch East Indies in early 1944.

On 23rd February 1944, at the Japanese South West Area Fleet Headquarters in Penang, under the command of Admiral TAKASU Shiro, a conference was held which planned an operation in the Indian Ocean to disrupt Allied lines of communication and supplies. It was code named Operation "Sayo No 1". Great emphasis was stressed upon secrecy. The operation was to be under the command of Rear-Admiral SAKONJU Naomasa 16th Squadron, with Captain SHIMANOUCHI Momochiyo as his Chief of Staff, the latter being summoned to attend the Penang conference. Later Takasu's headquarters were moved to Sourabaya where Lieutenant Commander KOYAMADA a staff officer of the 16th Squadron was summoned to discuss the operational plans and a detailed plan completed by the end of February. The capture of shipping was the primary purpose of the plan. In the written order, the sinking of vessels was not mentioned, but if the Allied ships tried to escape it was judged necessary to sink them. The "disposal" of prisoners of war was specified in the operational order issued by the South West Area Fleet Headquarters.

The Squadron was to comprise of three heavy cruisers, "AOBA", (flag ship) "CHIKUMA" and "TONE". The light cruisers "KINU" and "OI", three destroyers, "SHIKIMAMI", "URANAMI", and "AMARGIRI" forming a screen to escort the raiders out and back through the Sunda Strait. The South West Area Fleet also had the support of an air-force, but this was not under the control of the Rear-Admiral. Submarines from the 8th flotilla patrolled around Ceylon, the Maldives, and Chagos Archipelago.

Rear-Admiral Sakonju as Commander of the 16th Squadron, accepted his orders, and in turn issued them to vessels under his command. In his affidavit made on 16.4.47 he stated:

"I asked KOYAMADA the policy of headquarters and he replied – 'In view of the fact that the Allies are lately killing Japanese prisoners of war at GUADALCANAL by running tanks over them and are often bombing and torpedoing Japanese hospital ships, causing many casualties, the H.Q. came to a conclusion that the Allies are aiming at the reduction of Japan's man power, and H.Q. decided to retaliate' – I said 'Is that so!' I decided to accept the order to dispose of prisoner's of war. During the proceeding month, that is January, the light cruisers "KUMA" and "KITAGAMI" were sunk and heavily damaged by the enemy submarine action and many of my men were lost. The spirit of retaliation in fair combat was running high at that time among the officer's and men of the 16th Squadron".

The policy of killing as many survivors as possible had been applied by Japanese submarines earlier than 1944. In December 1943 the British ship "DAISY MOLLER", was sunk by submarine RO-110 and lifeboats carrying survivors rammed, followed by machine gun fire over a large area of water. In February 1944, the British ships "BRITISH CHIVALRY", "SUTLEJ" and "ASCOT", with survivors in the lifeboats and the water were subjected to similar treatment. In all these appalling cases there was heavy loss of life. In fact as early as January 1942 when the British ship "KWANTUNG" was sunk by a Japanese submarine, two lifeboats were sunk by ramming, and after the second attack only 13 of 98 crew were left alive. Many other similar atrocities committed by Japanese submarines to British, Dutch and American merchant seamen can be cited.

The "BEHAR" sailed from Melbourne on the 29th February 1944 with cargo loaded in New Zealand and Australia, bound for Bombay and Colombo, and by the morning of 9th of March was in the Indian Ocean several hundred miles to the southwest of Cocos Islands making a good speed.

On the 27th February, at Linga Captain MAYAZUMI of the cruiser "TONE" received the fleet operational order from the "AOBA", the flagship of 16th Squadron, issued and signed by Admiral Takasu, the Commander-in-Chief Southwest Area Fleet. In appendix 1 of this Order was a directive as to treatment of survivors of enemy ships sunk. All members of the crew and passengers were to be "disposed of" (killed) with the exception of Captain and part of the officers, as well as Radar, anti-submarine, W/T, and Aerial Operations personnel, who were to be picked up for interrogation. (This information was revealed by Captain Mayazumi in a sworn affidavit signed on 17.3.47). The ship left Linga for Bangka on the 27th. On the 28th Rear-Admiral Sakonju on board the "AOBA" decided details of the operation at a conference in the Bangka Straits. Ships within 200 miles of Cocos Islands were to be boarded by a prize crew, but ships outside this area were to be sunk.

The fleet sailed from the Bangka Straits that day, and passed through the Sunda Strait into the Indian Ocean on 1st March, where the three heavy cruisers "AOBA", "CHIKUMA" and "TONE" commenced their search for

Allied shipping without success until the 9th of March, when the "TONE" sighted a vessel which turned out to be the "BEHAR". The "TONE" was capable of 35 knots, having 8 eight inch guns and 8 five inch guns. This heavy armament was concentrated forward to keep the quarterdeck clear for the extensive aircraft arrangements, having on this occasion three aircraft stowed on board, although more could be carried.

PRISONERS OF WAR

The "BEHAR" was making good progress across the Indian Ocean following a course dictated by the routing instructions given to the Master by the naval authorities. The weather squally, frequent rain showers, which reduced visibility considerably, the wind being eastsoutheast with a moderate sea, and overcast sky. When one such rain squall had stopped and the visibility lifted, there appeared a warship which was recognised as a cruiser approaching on the "BEHAR's" starboard side, with guns trained on her. The "BEHAR" had been caught by surprise. Almost immediately the warship flashed an unrecognisable signal on the signalling lamp, which was repeated rapidly. Captain Symons ignored the signals, and turned the "BEHAR" away, and sounded the alarm bells, but immediately the warship broke out the Japanese battle ensign and opened fire from about 4,000 yards, registering hits on the second salvo both fore and aft. Fires started soon afterwards on the bridge, No. 1 hold, and on the poop, in addition the vessel started to list to starboard. Captain Symons ordered the Radio Officer to transmit a Raider Signal RRRR, followed by the ship's name and position. Within a few minutes it was obvious to all that "BEHAR" would not survive such heavy punishment for very much longer. Salvo followed salvo and in a few minutes the forward deck had collapsed. Captain Symons gave the order to abandon ship about five minutes after the action started. The order for the gunners on the "BEHAR" to open fire was never given. The engines were ordered to be stopped, the lifeboats prepared for launching. In the meantime, confidential papers had been thrown over the side in a weighted bag, the ASDIC apparatus stripped of detachable parts which also went into the sea.

By this time a second heavy cruiser had appeared on the port side of the "BEHAR", flying a flag at her masthead, which was later to be identified as an "Admiral's" flag. This vessel being the "AOBA", but it took no part in the shelling of the "BEHAR". It was remarkable in view of the punishment the vessel received that casualties were so light, particularly as the shelling was continuing as the vessel was being abandoned. However there was a lull of about five minutes when shelling stopped, the opportunity was taken to launch the life boats. Then the shelling re-commenced, and it was during the operation to get the lifeboats away that DEMS gunner A.B. Robinson, Royal Artillery gunner Pyecroft, and Indian rating Noor Khan were killed by shrapnel, but apart from those three no other deaths occurred due to that attack on the "BEHAR" by the "TONE". The "BEHAR" settled rapidly by the stern and capsized, the "TONE" closing in to finish the vessel off, finally sinking about 20 minutes after commencement of the attack.

In the abandonment of the vessel, although four boats were launched only three were used by the survivors, though not by all, some were in the water having jumped from the sinking vessel. The motor lifeboat engine would not start, and took fifteen minutes before it could be brought to life. The Japanese warship launched one of her own boats, picking up six or seven survivors which included Chief Officer, the 2nd Radio Officer and one gunner, whilst other lifeboats picked up the remainder who had jumped into the water. By this time the cruiser had approached nearer to the lifeboats, and had machine guns trained on the survivors. A voice in English ordered the lifeboats to come alongside the cruiser and get on board quickly, the threat of failing to heed the command was the stark alternative of being killed by machine gun fire.

As the lifeboats approached the cruiser, some of the

prisoners were able mentally to take notes of their attacker, some believing it was a six inch gun heavy cruiser, whilst others thought it had eight inch guns. At first glance the vessel appeared to have two small funnels, but in fact they joined together at the top as one. They had no idea of the identity of the cruiser, and in fact they were never to know this until well after the war finished, although the prisoners were to get clues which they passed on after liberation.

James Godwin a Royal New Zealand Navy Officer sailing as passenger gives the following version of the attack on the "BEHAR":

'When the ship was in mid-ocean between Ceylon and Australia and at about ten minutes to ten a.m. 9/3/44, while I was in the lounge I heard two loud explosions and on rushing outside I could see the ship was being shelled by a Japanese cruiser which was standing off about 2½ miles. The fire of the cruiser's 8 inch guns was directed on the ship. Several direct hits were registered on the "Behar". The cruiser ceased fire for a time during which those aboard the "Behar" made an attempt to abandon ship. This cessation of fire was about five minutes in duration after which the cruiser recommenced shelling from a distance of about 1500 yards. While the Captain of the ship (Capt Symons), the Third Officer, Barr and I were still aboard the shelling re-commenced. The lifeboats had then drifted away from either side of the "Behar" and we were compelled to jump into the water. As a result of the shelling a lot of those in the life-boats were wounded by shrapnel. The shelling was then at point blank range and no regard for the safety of the occupants of the lifeboats was shown.

The cruiser was either of "Aoba" or "Tony" class. Two other Japanese cruisers were in attendance. The "Behar" was equipped with one 4 inch gun but this did not come into action at all – it was out of action very early. Barr, the Captain and the Second Officer and I joined the same lifeboat. There were one or two Naval ratings, the ship's wireless operator (Walker), one cadet, and about 30

16

Lascars of the ship's crew in the lifeboat. Shells continued to fall after we joined the lifeboat. The Lascars were terror stricken and were useless with the result that about half a dozen of us were compelled to pull the boat.

The "Behar" was sinking when we left her. The shelling ceased at about 10.35 a.m. The cruiser responsible for the shelling circled around until the "Behar" sank, and later our boat was summoned to come alongside the cruiser. These orders were given by someone with a megaphone. The Captain of the "Behar" who was in charge of the lifeboat decided to go alongside. In all I saw three lifeboats manned. The occupants of all these lifeboats were ultimately taken aboard the cruiser. During the shelling I believe four were killed and many wounded'.

A jacob's ladder was lowered over the port quarter of the cruiser for survivors to climb up, and as each survivor reached the quarter deck, he faced a "firing squad" of about a dozen armed Japanese ratings under the command of a Japanese officer. Clothes, except shirts and trousers, were torn off them, shoes removed, plus any watches. Most of the prisoners were beaten severely by the guards on the quarter deck, under the instructions of officers strutting around with drawn swords. Each prisoner had his hands forced high behind his back, a rope tied to his wrist, then passed round his throat and back to the other wrist, being tied exceedingly tightly, to the point that if the prisoner tried to ease the pain in his arms by lowering them, he effectively started to choke himself with the rope tightening around his neck. Each survivor being ordered to squat on the deck, and not to speak to anyone. The 2nd Officer on reaching the quarter deck and being tied, was hit by a rating on the back of the head with a rifle butt on the instructions of the Japanese officer who spoke English. As a result of this beating, the 2nd officer fell to the deck, and because of the way he was tied he could not get up, received a second beating with a rifle butt. The Japanese officer then said in English "If you don't tell the truth you will be killed". One of the ladies, Mrs Pascheove, had trouble climbing the jacob's ladder, which delayed matters, but when she eventually reached the deck, was punched in the face by the Japanese Officer who spoke English.

After about two boat loads of survivors had got aboard, the Japanese officer was calling for the Captain to step forward, but he had not yet come on board. Later he asked again, and Captain Symons stood up and was marched across the deck. About half way across he was hit on the back of the head with the butt of a rifle, and fell to the deck, where he was dragged up and confronted by the English speaking officer who threatened that if he did not tell the truth he would be killed.

Captain Symons refused to answer any questions until the prisoners had their bonds released. The Officer said he could not do this, but had the ropes slackened a little, and in the case of the two ladies, they had their ropes removed. The prisoners were made to squat on the quarter deck of the cruiser under the blazing sun for about three hours, during which time they were beaten on their backs by Japanese naval ratings wielding bamboo sticks. After this period of time, following initial interrogation of the ship's officers and passengers, the prisoners still bound were forced below, down two decks, and confined in a small space about 36' x 15'.

Here they were made to sit crosslegged by the guard of about a dozen men, armed with wooden staves about five feet long. They were not allowed to talk or move, and any contravention of these orders resulted in an unmerciful beating, most prisoners being beaten even if they did sit correctly as required. One prisoner who came in for severe beatings, was the elderly retired passenger Mr Duncan MacGregor. He was beaten into unconsciousness on three occasions before the ship reached Java, because he could not maintain the cross legged position. Lieut S.C. Parker R.N.Z.N.V.R. a fellow passenger recorded in his affidavit:

'One survivor who was particularly badly beaten was a Mr. McGregor, a former Bank manager and member of

the Legislature in British East Africa. Apparently he was unable to squat in the Eastern fashion without support, and I saw him savagely beaten and kicked by the Japanese sailors, some of whom appeared to be of officer rank. Rifle butts, fists, and boots, were savagely used on McGregor by the Japanese sailors, who seemed to find amusement from this ill-treatment'.

Sergeant Ratcliffe an army gunner, was another to be so viciously beaten that he collapsed. Captain Green who was sailing as a passenger was to record later:

'The slightest movement of anyone and a staff would land with force on the head or body. My false teeth were broken with a blow. It was dark when eventually our ropes were taken off. We had been bound at least nine hours. A bowl of water was passed round, but we were allowed only a few sips each, some of us could not even hold the bowl. My hands were swollen to twice their size and a vivid blue, and wrists ringed with blood. The numbness did not leave my hands for two months'.

A.B. Angus Macleod of Stornoway, was to recall in his affidavit:

'There were six Japanese sentries in the room with us, some of them were armed with rifles and bayonets and sticks. We all got a beating with the sticks, but sentries seemed to have a particular spite against an old man name Macgregor who came from Glasgow, and was at one time manager of the Bank of India at Mombassa. This man would be about 63 years of age, and he found the greatest difficulty in sitting tailor fashion as the Japanese wanted him to, they beat him unmercifully about the head, body, and legs with the result that he was rendered unconscious on at least three occasions. An officer of the Fleet Air Arm Sub.Lieut. Godwin, a New Zealander, took pity on the old man and moved over close in order to support him with his knee. His move was seen by the Japanese sentries who gave him a *beating and moved him to another part of the room. An Indian saloon steward who appeared to be able to sit in the way in which the Japanese wanted him to, and who so far as I know did nothing wrong, was set about for no apparent reason and had his head split open with a stick by one of the sentries. The sentries then sent for the Japanese ship's doctor, who when he arrived bandaged the Indian's head and told the sentries to untie us. He then told us that we could lie down and said that he would see that we got something to eat. He returned to our room shortly afterwards with some Japanese ratings carrying biscuits and water which were distributed to us. After that all the whites were put in to the same room as the ship's officers, and the two women passengers. The Indian and Chinese members of the crew were left in the room which we had first occupied'.*

The following morning the interrogation of the European Officers, DEMS personnel, and passengers continued throughout the day. Mr Phillips the chief officer in an interview after repatriation with a company marine superintendent is recorded as stating, that the interrogations of Captain Symons, the 1st Radio Officer, and himself were very intense, and officers subjected to much intimidation:

'everything from offers of iced water to threats of decapitation being employed in the endeavour to obtain information'.

The prisoners were fed a small ball of rice three times a day, and given condenser water to drink, not freshwater, until a few days later, when a small quantity was provided, which the prisoners had to share out among themselves. Being in the tropics, and below decks, all the prisoners suffered badly from the heat and thirst. On the third day of captivity on board the cruiser, the prisoners were called on deck, and allowed to be in fresh air for half an hour, before being taken down below again, which became part of the routine for the day. All the time spent on the cruiser, the prisoners were not allowed to talk to one another, any infringement resulted in severe beatings. However with a little bit of freedom through being brought up on deck, and movement below decks, although guarded, the prisoners were able to observe their surroundings, and begin to pick up clues which were to help identify the vessel on which they were held prisoner. The number 102 appeared in various parts of the ship, and on deck three seaplanes were observed to carry this number, which suggested that they were on the vessel whose identity number was 102.

Three wooden toilets were rigged up on deck and over the side for the prisoners, one for the Europeans, one for the Indians, and one for the two women. Permission had to be asked to use the toilet. Sub. Lt. Godwin in his affidavit stated:

'On most occasions when going to the lavatory we had to pass between ranks of the Japanese crew who belaboured us with pieces of wood, flat edges of bayonets, fists and rifle butts. I suffered this on numerous occasions. Our hands were tied on every occasion we were allowed to proceed to the lavatory. I was savagely beaten whilst going to the lavatory on the 11th March 1944. It was dark and I was taken around the back of the convenience and beaten by a guard whose identity I don't know and other Japanese until I was practically unconscious. On this occasion a big piece of wood was used. After my beating on the 11th March, the Naval Surgeon aboard came down to have a look at us and when I pointed to the extensive injury to my head he just nodded and laughed'.

For the 104 prisoners on board the "TONE" their life had become sheer misery, in addition to the savage beatings, the torture of being cooped up in a baking steel oven below decks, without adequate water and un-palatable food, they had the fear of the unknown: where were they going? what was to become of them?

After the sinking of the "BEHAR", the Japanese,

fearful that their presence in the Indian Ocean would be known because of the "Raider" signal transmitted by her, decided to return to the Sunda Straits and Batavia. According to the affidavit made by Captain Mayazumi on 17.3.47 in Stanley Gaol, Hong Kong, the "TONE" rejoined the "AOBA" at 1400 hours and reported by signal (this would be to the effect that he had 104 survivors on board). Whereupon he received a signal from the Senior Staff Officer Commander Shimanouchi of the 16th Squadron, to treat persons captured in accordance with Fleet Operational Order. "Dispose of them immediately in accordance with Order". Mayazumi replied that the prisoners were in the process of being interrogated. Not only was Captain Mayazumi greatly troubled by this order to "dispose of the prisoners", but also his first Lieutenant Commander Mii was also against carrying out this barbaric command. In the afternoon of the following day the 10th of March, Mayazumi signalled to Rear-Admiral Sakonju proposing the prisoners should not be killed, but Englishmen be used for construction of airfields and Indians used as crews for small motor barges. Sakonju replied from the "AOBA" with a signal that read approximately "Meirei Dori Tadachi ni Shobun Seyo" – "Dispose of them immediately in accordance with order". Again Mayazumi decided not to comply with the order, and proposed to try again to save the prisoners lives when the 16th Squadron reached Batavia. By now the interrogation of the prisoners was completed, having being conducted by Lieut. (Pay) Nagai the English speaking officer.

By the 13th March the Squadron was about 200 miles off the Cocos Islands and becoming fearful that aircraft from carriers based in Ceylon would be on patrol looking for them. Captain Mayazumi was apprehensive that if the ship came under attack, when all his crew would be required for battle stations, there would be a problem of maintaining guard of the prisoners. According to Mayazumi, below the prisoners there were a number of damage control valves, and as the Europeans were experienced seafarers, he considered if they got loose through being unguarded, they could do great damage to the ship. His other misgiving being that if the ship should sink, and prisoners escaped and were rescued by the Allies, they would be in a position to give away valuable information, and on this point the secret operational order was quite emphatic. Whilst rounding the Cocos Islands, Commander Mii reported to his Captain that numerous radio signals and electrical impulses were intercepted from Ceylon and Australia, which probably meant that enemy forces were approaching and all the officers on board were becoming uneasy. Some officers thought that the order to dispose of the prisoners should be carried out, but most agreed with their Captain and First Lieutenant that the order should not be carried out. Fresh water was becoming scarce, and all the fresh food had been consumed, but Mayazumi informed his officers and crew that he was determined to make Batavia with the prisoners on board. The "AOBA" was an older smaller vessel with smaller bunker capacity compared to the "TONE", and only capable of 15 knots which gave Mayazumi further concern.

On the 15th March, the squadron anchored off Tandjong Priok the port for Batavia, the capital of Java, and, of what was once the Dutch East Indies. The vessels arrived at 1900 hours Tokyo time, which was about one hour before sunset local time. What followed next is best quoted directly from the affidavit of Captain Mayazumi:

'I immediately went on board the flagship and reported that the prisoners had not been killed and that in my opinion should not be killed but made to work as suggested previously. For this suggestion I was rebuked by two staff officers (Shimanouchi and Oyamada). The commander of the squadron understood my feelings but because of the Fleet Order, could not change his decision. I experienced a sense of failure but determined to try once again on the next day at a gathering of officers. I was ordered to send the Master of the "Behar" and 2 or 3 others to the flagship for further interrogation.

I understood that the 2 women were not to be included in this number, so tried to persuade Rear-Admiral Sakonju to save them, as it was pitiful to treat them as prisoners. He asked me if there was anything suspicious about them, as women do not travel in wartime unless they were on a military mission. He permitted me to include the women when I told him that there was absolutely nothing suspicious about them. I ordered the Chief Paymaster who had conducted the interrogation to include as many prisoners as possible in the number to be sent to the flagship, and I personally indicated the persons concerned. As far as I can remember the following 16 persons were on the list – 2 women, Master, Chief Engineer, Chief Officer, 2nd Officer, Radio Officer, Dr Ching, a naval AB probably an anti-submarine rating, 1 army gunner, 1 petty officer D.C., 1 petty officer anti-submarine, 2 N.C.O. RNZAF, 1 petty officer radar and the Master of a ship which had rescued Japanese air pilots in the China Sea in September 1937".

On the 16th March the prisoners went up on deck for exercise, and found themselves in port. Captain Green recognised the surroundings as Batavia, and the word passed round. Also to be seen was another heavy cruiser which carried the Admiral's flag. Around midday when the prisoners were fed their by now customary ball of rice, they were visited by the Japanese Marine Officer who had done the interrogating, plus two other officers. This officer then called out the following names: Captain Symons, Chief Mate Phillips, Chief Engineer Weir, Chief Radio Officer Walker, Petty Officer Griffiths, A.B.s Kershaw and Macleod, Captain Green, the Royal New Zealand Navy Officers, Parker, Benge and Godwin. The Royal New Zealand Flight Sergeant, the Chinese Doctor, and the two lady passengers Mrs Pascheove and Mrs Shaw. The prisoners were then taken up on deck, leaving behind the remaining Europeans, and never to see them again. All the Indian and Chinese crew were at this stage also left on board. Petty Officer Griffiths reported: 'our request for our footwear to be returned was refused'. Captain Green the Merchant Navy captain sailing as a passenger, reported that after the names were called out, the prisoners were warned by a Japanese Officer who made a speech that they must be obey orders or they would be killed. Captain Green claimed in his affidavit that this officer was Rear Admiral Sakonju, who he identified in a parade at Stanley Gaol, Hong Kong. However it would seem Captain Green must have been mistaken in this identity, as no record can by found of the Admiral visiting the "TONE" in Tandjong Priok Roads. On that particular day, a staff conference was being held on the "AOBA" reviewing the recent operations.

Captain Mayazumi in his affidavit concerning the transfer of prisoners stated he:

'felt anxious as the number was about 3 times that asked by the Staff Officer. I knew that the lady prisoners were given back their passports, cheque books, and other papers. I found that the others who were taken to the flagship were wearing rings etc., and was satisfied that nothing had been taken away from them. A full list of the captured persons on forms prescribed by the Fleet was sent to the flagship.'

As the prisoners left their prison ship, they were able to look back and note details of its appearance, that all the main armament was forward, torpedo tubes amidships, the after deck was clear for the stowage of the sea planes, and the two small funnels joined at the top as one. They also were able to see that their "new prison ship" flying an Admiral's flag, was considerably different from their last one, having heavy armament on the after deck. Both ships appeared to have been painted black, but now looked rusty and dirty, obviously showing signs that it was a long time since they were in drydock.

However for the prisoners still remaining on board, they must have been wondering what was going to happen to them, possibly thinking that those leaving the ship were being taken ashore for further interrogation in view of their rank aboard ship, or in the case of service and Merchant Navy personnel sailing as passengers, their knowledge would also be of interest to the Japanese intelligence services. The ship's officers of the "BEHAR" left on board the "TONE" being the 2nd, 3rd, and 4th Deck Officers, the two Apprentices Denys J. Mathews aged 17, Alan Moore aged 18 and all the Engineer Officers with the exception of the Chief Engineer. Of the crew, 41 Indian and 2 Chinese crew remained together with 12 service personnel who manned the guns and Asdic apparatus. The elderly passenger Mr. MacGregor also remained on board the "TONE". None of these prisoners would have had any idea what the Japanese were planning to do with them, and probably surmised they would be landed later, or taken on to another port.

The 15 prisoners selected to be taken off the "TONE" were transferred to the flagship of the 16th Squadron,the "AOBA", where they were separated and imprisoned in various parts of the ship, but one group consisting of Captain Green, Chief Officer Phillips, Chief Radio Officer Walker, Petty Officer Griffiths, the Chinese Doctor, and A.B. Macleod were kept together in a small room. James Godwin, who had suffered particularly badly on the "TONE" was placed in solitary confinement, and recorded that the food was still bad. The prisoners were still not allowed to talk to each other, and the various groups did not come into contact with each other, although on the whole had a little more freedom of movement and could go on deck when they wished. They also had more rice to eat, and were allowed to wash every morning.

At the conference of 16th March, Captain Mayazumi again brought up the subject of the captured prisoners, but was given the same answers:

'Afterwards I was asked by SHIMANOUCHI and OYAMADA to explain my course from Batavia to Singapore and they studied soundings and distance from

shore and directed that when I was more than 40 miles from land with a sounding of more than 20 fathoms in open sea I was to carry out the execution. SHIMANOUCHI repeated these instructions to Rear-Admiral SAKONJU and when I again protested to Sakonju he said, " I understand your position but the orders are from the C-in-C in his Operational Order for operational purposes and you <u>must</u> act as you have been instructed". I felt this was a very definite order. On the 16th evening, I was invited to a dinner given by Lt.Gen. HARADA the Army Officer commanding Batavia and on the 17th I went to a dinner given by the Senior Naval Officer, Capt. MAEDA and at these functions could not discuss the captured persons question with Sakonju and I knew that I had failed'.

Mayazumi continues with his affidavit:

'On 17.3.44 while at lunch at a Japanese restaurant in Batavia with GOTO Gonzo, a retired Naval Captain, at the time connected with the Batavia branch of the Kawasaki Dockyard, my executive officer Commander Mii, reported to me that Admiral Sakonju had refused to entertain a proposal to obtain permission to land prisoners. Commander Mii met Rear Admiral Sakonju at the residence of Mr YOSHIOKA, the Senior Civil Officer at the Naval Headquarters. The proposal was put up to the Rear Admiral who then gave permission to land a few Indians but no others. I commended Mii for his efforts and ordered him to send as many as possible ashore as I had previous engagements to look over Captain Goto's dockyards and to attend Capt. Maeda's dinner and could not get back to the Tone. After this dinner Comdr. Mii informed me that SHIMANOUCHI would not change the order and I had another interview with Rear-Admiral SAKONJU, and repeated my request for the order to be changed but he refused'.

During the Military Trial in 1947 Commander MII gave his version of events. He stated that he went ashore to meet the Commander CHIBA Katsuo of the Cruiser "OI", which had also returned to Batavia (Tandjong Priok) to plead with him to speak to Rear-Admiral Sakonju to save the prisoners, and on the night of the 16th March MII with Mr YOSHIOKA appealed to the Admiral to have all the prisoner's landed.

MARCH 18TH 1944

On the 18th March the 15 prisoners held on the "AOBA" were landed ashore and taken by lorry to Batavia and put in a medium size room at the Naval Barracks, where their conditions were a little better in that in the room was a basin and tap. The two ladies were given a room of their own next to the men.

Captain Mayazumi arrived on board the "TONE" at 1400 hours on the 18th March, where he was handed a signal authorising the landing of about ten Indians, and was informed that twenty had been landed whilst he was ashore: Mii surmised that the Commander of the Squadron had thought that no leakage of information would result from the transfer of a few uneducated Indian seaman ashore. The "TONE" and the heavy cruiser "CHIKUMA" were under orders to sail later that day for Singapore with Captain NORIMITSU as the senior officer of the Division. The Japanese considered the Java Sea was unsafe due to submarines and aircraft operating from the Indian Ocean. Entrances to Tandjong Priok and Bangka Straits were dangerous submarine zones. Mayazumi's affidavit of 17.3.47:

'The execution could not be carried out in the Bangka Straits as we could be seen from the shores. It was decided that the best place was about 40 or 50 miles from Batavia. I delayed the order for the execution as I had hopes that there would be a change in the situation, or that I may be ordered to transfer the prisoners to a cargo ship or transport. I regret no such change materialised. At 2200 hours Tokyo time, 3 hours before reaching Bangka Straits, I transmitted the Admiral's order

to Lt. Ishihara. At about 1700 hours Tokyo time, before we left Batavia, I told Lt. Ishihara that I had orders to carry out the execution. The method of execution was to see that it was carried out with least possible pain and suffering and it was suggested that the execution should take place at night. The prisoners were taken out one by one as if for further interrogation, then knocked unconscious and killed while still in that state. The execution must be carried out by a well educated graduate of the Naval College so as to avoid cruelty, and so that there would be no failure due to lack of knowledge of the weapon used. Courteous treatment of the bodies was ordered. A sword was to be thrust through the heart to assure death. The use of fire-arms forbidden because of flash and sound. All this was explained to me by OYAMADA on 16.3.44. Just before reaching Bangka Straits I received a report from Ishihara that the execution had been carried out in accordance with OYAMADA's suggestion. I heard a sword had been used to cut the jugular vein and a thrust was made into the heart to ensure against failure. There were several members in the execution party but I can only remember the names of two officers: Sub Lt. KINOSHITA and Acting Sub Lt. YOSHIOKA. I did not witness the execution as I was on the bridge all the time. I erased the record of the signals in the signals record book, referring to the prisoners and the execution from the reports sent to the 16th Squadron, 7th Squadron and the Southwest Fleet, in case the book should fall into enemy hands. I sent a written report of the execution to SAKONJU's and TAKASU's H.Q.s. In May 1944, Shimanouchi and Oyamada informed me in Singapore that they had received these written reports.'

PRISONERS IN JAVA AND JAPAN

Ashore at the Naval Barracks in Batavia the prisoners were allowed to speak to one another, and were given mats to lie on and issued with a small bar of soap every second day, as well as getting half an hour's exercise in a field behind the barracks every day. They were also issued with a shirt and a pair of trousers. Whilst no further beatings were inflicted, the food ration was very meagre. Twenty of the Indian crew turned up at the camp, and were placed in an adjoining room to the surprise of the other prisoners, who up to then had no idea what had become of those left on board, in fact they were not to know in some cases the answer until many years after the war had ended. Mr Griffiths never knew the truth until 1956. It appears that the Indian crew, on arrival at Tandjong Priok Roads, were put to work getting rice and vegetables on board cruiser 102 (TONE) from a barge, all the stores being marked "102". When this ship was loaded, the remaining stores marked "104" were loaded aboard another cruiser. Upon their arrival at the Naval barracks, the Europeans and Indians were not allowed to speak to one another.

On April 18th the European party were split up for further interrogation by the Kem Pei Tei the Japanese Gestapo, and kept in solitary confinement for ten days. Mr Phillips the Chief Officer reported in November 1945 to his company's Marine Superintendent at Cardiff, that the interrogations were conducted without brutality of any description, blandishment in the form of iced drinks, cigarettes, sweets, etc., being used. However Angus Macleod the Royal Navy Asdic Operator gives a different version of events as he recalled them after arriving at the Naval Barracks.

'At the end of a week the women were taken away. After another seven days had passed, all the whites and the Chinese Doctor were taken to a house in the centre of Batavia. This house was owned by a Japanese Naval Commander. There the Chief Mate, the Chief Engineer, Sub Lieut. GODWIN, P.O.GRIFFITHS, Flight Sergeant BARR, and KERSHAW, were sent to another house in Batavia, leaving Captain GREEN, our own Captain, two of the Fleet Air Arms Officers, the Chinese Doctor, the two women and myself in the house. The two women were given a room in the house, in which was a bed,

blankets and a mosquito net, and they appeared to be well treated. The rest of us were housed in the stables and three of us shared a stall. Our guard was an Indian civilian who spoke good English, and he did his best to get us more food than our ration. We were allowed three meals per day, consisting of plenty of rice, and a bowl of soup each time. Our Indian guard, however, managed to get us sweet potatoes, an odd cup of tea, and even supplied us with a razor and blades, and a book each. We remained more or less unmolested for about fourteen days, during which time we sat about and read. At the end of that time, six Army Officers all in the same Japanese Army uniform, arrived at the house and began interrogating us.

Each officer took one man in turn for interrogation. As soon as the first officer had finished with us, the second officer began his part of the questioning. This went on every day from 09.00 hours until 1800 hours, and on one occasion I was sent for at about 21.00 hours and kept for two hours, during which time I was questioned as to the cargo on the "BEHAR" carried from Karachi to Calcutta. This was cement and rice, and the Japanese wanted to know what the cement was for. On the second or third day of interrogation, I was asked by one officer which was the strongest navy in the world. I told him it was the British Navy. On this occasion there was a Japanese sentry in the room along with us. As soon as I said this, the officer nodded to the sentry who then gave me a blow on the back of the neck with the butt of his rifle. The unexpected nature of the blow caused me to fall, though the blow itself was not a hard one. I was then asked which was the second strongest navy in the world and I answered, "The Americans". The officer gave another nod and I got a second blow from the sentry on the back of the neck. I was expecting it and this time I did not fall. I was then asked if that, in the event of the British home fleet joining up with Admiral Summerville, I thought that along with the Americans they could defeat the Japanese Navy. By this time I was getting wise to the game and I replied that I didn't think they would. The officer then said: "That's right. You're getting some sense now." Interrogation lasted in all for nine days, but this was the only instance of ill-treatment which I suffered during that time'.

A. B. Kershaw recalls that he was interrogated by Japanese Naval Intelligence Officers who spoke English with an American accent. They were interested in ports that the "BEHAR" had called at, wanting descriptions of entrances, general topography, and state of the waters, whether clear, muddy, shark infested etc., which he gave answers to, but knowing they were wrong. Captain Green recorded that:

'after a month at the naval barracks, six of them were taken to the house of an intelligence officer and lodged in stables at the end of the garden. I told him what had happened to my teeth and he had them repaired for me. We were questioned almost daily for six weeks, however my concoction of a story was easy to stick to, there being no else to trip me up. Our fare here was much better to begin with, but it gradually dropped off. I was amazed to find they had no interest in the merchant service codes, it appeared they could decipher them as soon as a new one came out, though they could not make anything of the navy codes to date'.

Notes made by Chief Officer Phillips after the war ended, details the dates that his group, consisting of Chief Engineer Weir, Flt.Sgt Barr, A.B. Kershaw A.B. Macleod, Petty Officer Griffiths, and Doctor Lee were split up in solitary confinement from April 18–28th for interrogation by Kem Pei Tei. (It should be noted other prisoners considered they were interrogated by army or naval intelligence officers). Macleod then recalls in his affidavit:

'We remained in these quarters for a further fortnight, and then we were taken back to the Naval Barracks in Batavia. On our return, we found that one of the Indians had died from an attack of dysentery. Other three were affected and were receiving no treatment from the Japanese. Within four hours we were all moved again, this time to a camp in Batavia which had formerly been the headquarters of the 10th Battalion Dutch Militia. It is situated in Hospital Street, Batavia. On arrival we were placed in cells. The three Indians affected with dysentery, and three companions occupied one cell, while about sixteen of us forming the remainder, occupied another small cell. Our Captain, Captain Green, the Chief Wireless Operator, and the three Fleet Air Arm Officers were kept behind at the barracks, and the two women were sent to a women's camp in Batavia'.

The Chief Officers group met briefly with Captain Symons on May 21st at the Naval Barracks, before being handed over to the Japanese Military and placed in dark cells at P.O.W. No 1 camp Batavia.

Captain Green describes what followed next after interrogation and return to the naval barracks of himself, Captain Symons, Chief Radio Officer Walker, Lt. Parker, Sub. Lt. Benge and Sub. Lt Godwin:

'We were taken by train to Sourabaya, handed over to the naval authorities there who put us straight away into cells like criminals, worse, as we were put in three's into a single cells. We were not allowed a wash in the eighteen days we were there, and they often did not trouble to bring us food, sometimes only a little rice and a few shreds of sour cabbage once in a whole day. We were then taken out, blindfolded, handcuffed, tied to a leader rope, then put on a truck, driven to the docks and put on board a transport with a guard of six men to accompany us to Japan' (The prisoners were in fact placed aboard the "SANUKI MARU", for the voyage to Japan via Singapore.) 'I could not describe the horror of the trip (via Singapore). My legs were beginning to swell with Beriberi. Malnutrition was visible in all of us, certainly we were in no fit shape for rough handling. We were never visited by an officer and those sadistic *maniacs beat us up daily. Our handcuffs were not removed day or night for three weeks. They were the narrow American self-gripping type and used for an added torture'.*

The nightmare voyage to Japan for the six prisoners was the subject of a sworn affidavit concerning ill-treatment made by the Chief Radio Officer, Arthur C.R. Walker of Greenford Middlesex. The following paragraphs are extracts of his affidavit:

'3. We were accommodated two in a cabin and to start with I was with BENGE. For the majority of the voyage GODWIN and I shared a cabin.

4. Seven guards had been detailed to escort us – six Petty Officers and one Leading Seaman – of whom one was in charge of the party. For the first two or three days treatment under the circumstances was fairly reasonable and so was the food we received (by Japanese standards).

5. As time went on, however, it was apparent that there was one Petty Officer who was out to make himself unpleasant to us. It is very difficult to give a description of him as he had no outstanding physical characteristics, being only of medium size, but it was evident that he was a pretty hardened character. He was, I think, judging by his badges, of the lowest rank of Petty Officer, but above his badges of rank he wore on his sleeve a red chrysanthemum.

6. For the whole of the voyage we were handcuffed and it became the practice to make us do "exercises" once a day. These exercises consisted solely of making us get into the "press up" position on the floor of the cabin and remaining, still handcuffed, with our arms in that position for long periods – anything up to 20 minutes at a time. As soon as we showed sign of tiring, this particular Petty Officer, who was out to make trouble for us, used to hit us with a bamboo stick or with knotted rope's end. This practice became a daily occurrence for the rest of the voyage with the consequence that both GODWIN and myself were covered with bruises and welts. As regards myself, I think that as I was fairly small I got off comparatively lightly. GODWIN, however, being a big man was very badly beaten up the whole time, both on the face and body and on the legs. He was in fact so badly beaten on his legs that he had great difficulty at times in walking. Although the particular Japanese I have already referred to in paragraph 5 above was the one who usually carried out these beatings, the Leading Seaman also used to beat us up on occasions, I think merely with the idea of impessing his companions.

7. Another form of ill-treatment to which we were subjected by the ring-leader I have described in paragraph 5, was to make us kneel right back on our heels with our bodies bolt upright and to hold out in front of us at arms length, a heavy porthole cover. This also was for long periods at a time and as soon as we showed signs of tiring he used to hit us under the arms with a bamboo stick.

8. The Petty Officer in charge of the escort knew perfectly well what was going on and took no action to stop it, except on one occasion when the ring-leader hit GODWIN particularly hard across the face with the bamboo stick and cut him open just above the eye. On this occasion the Petty Officer in charge did call a halt for the day.

9. During the course of the voyage I used to see Captain SYMONS and Lieutenant PARKER in the wash place. It was obvious that they must have been particularly brutally beaten up as their faces were swollen up enormously. I did not, however, get a chance to talk to them. We were never allowed to go on deck except to go to the latrine which was a wooden structure at the aft end of the ship.

10. As the voyage went on, the food gradually became less in quantity, so that eventually we were only getting a small bowl of rice and barley, and a few scraps of pickled cabbage three times a day.

11. When we arrived at OSAKA we were escorted by the same guards on the tram and train to OFUNA Interrogation Camp. The voyage lasted for about three to four weeks.

12. I am certain that I should be able to recognise photographs of all the seven of the escort if they were shown to me.'

With the prisoners now arrived at Osaka, the letter written by Captain Green to his employer's, Messrs John Swire & Sons, London from his hospital bed in New Zealand following repatriation gives a harrowing account of his captivity in Japan:

'On arrival at Osaka, we were taken ashore at night and trammed to Kobe and sent by train to Ofuna (15 miles from Yokohama). We had about three miles to walk to the camp. It was a very hot day, our feet blistered on the hot road, our features hardly recognisable, so swollen with punching, and our bodies black and blue with bruises. In addition, I had a broken rib from a kick, and my legs and feet were an abnormal size due to Beriberi and strain from being strung up with ropes. The guards made us carry their baggage although handcuffed.

Ofuna was an unregistered questioning camp containing about eighty men, most of them being young American Pilots. Everything was done to humiliate the men and break their morale. No difference was made between Officers and Ratings. Public floggings were usual for most paltry offences and so severe that I have seen men faint when forced to watch the beatings of their friends. The guards were the biggest and toughest Japanese that I have ever seen – no doubt specially picked for the job. Soon after my arrival I was picked on for not being able to follow some of the complicated rhythm of their Swedish drill, and I was obliged to stand out while a guard beat me with both fists and smashed my false teeth to pieces. The food here was foul. A small bowl of so-called soup (usually turnip water) and one of barley, usually half cooked, stinking with age and some of it blue with mildew, were provided at each meal. It played havoc with our bowels and I suffered constantly for a whole year. It also needed a good deal of chewing, which I was unable to do and it wasn't long before I started to vomit daily. My ears started to discharge, a complaint I had before but had not had a sign of for twelve years, no doubt brought on again by the punchings I had received. I also suffered from frequent abscesses.

I was kept in the Ofuna Camp exactly three months, then with thirty others, was taken to the Omari headquarters camp. A couple of days later, Capt. Symons (of the "BEHAR"), his Wireless Operator and a dozen ratings were sent off to one of the mines. I was able to stay behind only because of illness, there being two American Doctors there as well as a Japanese student (in charge). My weight was then sixty kilos – 51lbs less than normal.

The Japanese do not recognise the Merchant Navy, or treat Officers as such. I was put in a shed of about 60ft x 20ft. with two six foot wide wooden shelves on each side. On these shelves over a hundred ate and slept. A space was made for me between a private in the Middlesex Regiment and a Navy stoker. Space was carefully marked off, twenty-nine inches of shelf per man. I was given two pieces of rice sacking for a mattress (a little better than the stone floors of Java). The Officers had four small cubicles at the ends of the shed. The floor was mud, and there was no heating of any kind with a winter temperature of ten to fifteen degrees below freezing. Opposite me was a young man, both of his legs amputated due to Beriberi. Quite near to me were two more – all their toes had dropped off. Most men had

Palagra of the eyes, etc., and all could tell of friends who had died.

I had to go out with the men to the Shobura goods yard – loading railway trucks – carrying sacks of rice up planks and stacking in godowns. I frequently reported sick but had to carry on working. Harbour work was supposed to be easier, – down the holds of filthy tramp steamers, discharging pig iron.

The American doctors eventually got the Japs to agree to put me on the "permanent sick" list to work in the camp leather shop. The food became worse and I would often vomit it whilst attempting to eat it, and the continual pain I suffered was indescribable. Many men, since then, have frankly admitted that they did not expect me to live through the winter. I owe everything to a man named Millard (of Dover), who knew my brother by sight and at first mistook me for him. He worked in the cookhouse and whenever possible, at considerable risk to himself, would steal some of the guards' food for me.

On the 30th May, three hundred of us were sent to a new camp in the mountains about fifty miles west of Sendai to work in the pig-iron and carbide factory. "Slave" – not "work" is a better word. Ten percent of the men were "permanent sick." We were called "Gardeners" and were out of camp eleven to fourteen hours a day in all weather, clearing virgin land of dense scrub, tree roots and rocks with the crudest of native implements.

It is surprising how men in such poor condition could stick it, but the constant fear of being clubbed with the butt of a rifle or beaten by the guards kept us going. There were no "rest days" as in Omari, there we had every alternate Sunday off".

After the Japanese Capitulation, I was taken to a hospital in Morioka by the Swiss Consul, later put aboard H.M.H.S. "Tjitjalengka" and finally landed in Auckland as a stretcher case.

I appeal to you, Mr. Swire, to get the ship owners whose officers were captured by the Japanese, to request our Government to sue the Japanese Government for adequate compensation for not treating *us as civilians or officers, and forcing us to work and live as private soldiers'.*

The following information was provided by John Swire & Sons, London, from their files, sadly much depleted following re-organisation over the years in London and Hong Kong.

THIS IS TO CERTIFY THAT CAPTAIN PERCY JAMES GREEN, BRITISH MERCHANT MARINE, CAPTURED ON THE INDIAN OCEAN MARCH 9TH 1944. ARRIVED AT THE HEADQUARTERS CAMP OF THE TOKYO PRISONER-OF-WAR AREA ON 29TH SEPTEMBER 1944. HE WAS DETAINED THERE AS A PRISONER-OF-WAR BY THE JAPANESE ARMY, RECEIVING THE SAME TREATMENT IN EVERY RESPECT AS A PRIVATE SOLDIER, BEING FORCED TO DO COMMON LABOUR AT THE SHIBAURA RAILWAY YARD IN TOKYO CITY. FOR REASONS OF CONTINUED ILL HEALTH HE WAS LATER ASSIGNED BY THE JAPANESE AUTHORITIES TO EMPLOYMENT ON LEATHER WORK IN A SHOP WITHIN THE CAMP.
ON MAY 30TH, 1945, HE WAS TRANSFERRED TO A BRANCH PRISONER-OF-WAR CAMP AT WAKASENNIN IN THE SENDAI AREA, WHERE SIMILAR TREATMENT WAS ACCORDED. HE WAS THERE ONE OF A FEW MEN EXCUSED HEAVY WORK AT THE IRON MILL BUT CLASSIFIED AS A GARDENER AND EMPLOYED FOR THE MOST PART FOR LONG HOURS CLEARING SCRUB LAND FOR CULTIVATION. THROUGHOUT, NO PRIVILEGES OR RECOGNITION WERE ACCORDED TO CAPTAIN GREEN BY THE JAPANESE.

(SIGNED) F.H. FRANKCOM, Major
ARMY EDUCATIONAL CORPS
OFFICER COMMANDING
ALLIED TROOPS AT CAMP
10 D. SENDAI
WAKASENNIN JAPAN   26th August 1945

Whilst the six prisoners sent to Japan suffered, the remaining prisoners in Java suffered likewise. Sometime in June 1944 the Chinese Doctor of Agriculture Lai Yung Li (Lei Lai Yung?) was taken away from the P.O.W. camp and was never seen again. The Goanese Butler Joao Santan Continho, age 63, died in May 1944, being taken from the Naval Barracks Batavia in a dying condition. Fireman Jooma Khan Kamroodeen died of dysentery on 21st May 1944 at the Naval Barracks, and the Deck Serang Hoossein Beelal died of the same disease at the Del Rosea hospital on 27th May 1944.

The affidavit given by the Hebridean sailor Angus Macleod is particularly informative and articulate about camp life of the "BEHAR" survivors in Java:

'Our Captain, Captain GREEN, the Chief Wireless Operator, and the three Fleet Air Arm Officers were kept behind at the barracks, and the two women were sent to a women's camp in Batavia. I afterwards learned that our Captain and his companions were sent to Japan. About half an hour after our arrival, an Artillery Officer of the British Army, who had been taken prisoner when Java fell, brought us a basket of rice, a four-gallon petrol tin of soup, another similar tin containing tea, and a loaf of bread weighing about half a pound. Part of this food was provided by the camp authorities and the remainder paid for out of a Pool voluntarily subscribed by Allied Officers, themselves prisoners in Japanese hands. We were so hungry and starved by this time, that all we could look at was the soup and the bread, and we managed to drink some tea.

About half an hour after we had finished our meal, the senior Medical Officer in the camp, Major O'Donnell, of the R.A.M.C., also taken in Java, came to see the Indians, he conferred with the Camp Commandant, and the result was that they were removed to the outside hospital the following morning. At the outside hospital were Lieut. Col. MAISIE, of the R.A.M.C., and Captain GILLIES of the Australian Medical Corps. The following morning, about 07.30 hours, we were allowed out for a wash, but was warned that we were not to speak to any other prisoner except those who had come in with us. We remained in the cells all that day and the following day. The food was quite good and we got a cup of tea in addition to our usual meals, at 20.00 hours. I afterwards found out that the tea was given on the orders of the Camp Commandant, who, as there was a plentiful supply of tea, gave us this to drink instead of water from which we might have contracted dysentery.

At the end of the second day, we were all shifted from the cells and taken to the camp stables. Twenty-two of us, Indians and whites alike, were housed in the former stables of the 10th Battalion Dutch Militia. The stalls had been removed, and for the first night we slept on the stone floor. We had plenty of room. One part of the stables was used as a rice store. On the second night there, we were provided with two straw mats each, and this made up our bed and bedding for the next ten months. The daily routine was that at 07.30 hours we were wakened by the bugle and roll called. After that we were allowed to visit the lavatories, and on our return we got a cup *(unreadable text at this point)* hours the guard there were two on all the time at our hut — changed, and there was roll-call again. From then until 12.00 hours all we could do was walk up and down the floor, sit about, and converse with one another. At 12.00 hours we got rice and soup and a cup of tea. This cup of tea was provided by our own officers, and we had to keep it for the sake of a drink in between this meal and next one which came at 18.00 hours. This meal consisted of soup and a slice of bread, and we kept half of the bread for our breakfast next morning. At 20.00 hours we had another cup of tea. For the first week we did not get out at night, but afterwards we were allowed out to walk on the road outside the stables for about an hour, during which time we were not allowed to speak to anybody we might meet.

About a month after we were in, some of the Koreans, who acted as guards on the camp, and were in the habit of getting drunk at nights, used to come into the stables and beat us with bamboo poles. These guards could not get into the camp and do this without being seen by the officers, but they could get into the stables without anyone knowing. This sort of thing would sometimes happen twice a day, and on occasions, we might be a month without interference. On one occasion, the Indian Engine-room Serang, who was a man of some sixty years, had his teeth knocked out by one of these Koreans. I, personally, suffered the same as the rest and was beaten up once or twice, but none of us suffered severe injury, apart from the Indian. One of the Koreans, whose name was "KARNEKO", tried to stop this conduct, and was eventually involved in a fight which resulted in the Kempei taking him away. We did not see him again. The Kempei – the Japanese Gestapo – had their Headquarters just a short distance from the camp. About this time we learned of an effort on the part of Wing Commander NICHOLLS, himself a prisoner and the senior Allied Officer on the camp, to get us out of the stables. This effort was unsuccessful. About ten days later, all the Allied Officers, with exception of a few to run the camp, were shifted to Bandoeng. About the same time, the Japanese Commandant was shifted to the women's camp and his place taken by Lieutenant KEROSHIMA.

Whether because our officers had left the camp or because of some action by the new Commandant, I do not know, but our rations became much less from then onwards. When Wing Commander NICHOLLS had left, Lieut. HAYES, of the R.A.S.C., had taken over and he tried to get us outside on work on the gardens, where there were some spinach beds. By this time our number in the stables had grown. A former German pilot and some Dutch half-castes had joined us. It was arranged that twenty of our number would be allowed every alternate day to work on the spinach. We were also informed that we would require to pay five cents each for a bar of soap and this was the reason why HAYES tried to get us out on work of some kind, for which we were paid ten cents a day. This continued for about four months.

During this time living conditions in the stables were gradually getting worse. We had no change of clothing, and both our bodies and our clothing were verminous. Lice and bugs were our chief trouble, and although Major O'DONNELL tried to obtain our clothing for delousing, his efforts met with no response, so that we were in a sorry plight. In addition, rats abounded in the stables, and during the night they would be running over us as we lay on the floor. Then we got wooden tables and trestles to sleep on, but these were also vermin-ridden and in spite of our efforts with hot water and anything else we could get, matters remained just as bad.

Two of the Indians had Malaria and were only able to get small doses of quinine which, although certainly helped towards their recovery, were not sufficient for their needs. Another six Dutch half-castes had joined us, and each one suffered from scabies. They were bad cases and were kept in a part of the stable shut off from us by barbed wire. A Dutch Medical Orderly came down and painted their bodies with stuff like varnish, which, in time, cured them. While this was going on, there were more arrivals to our stables, until finally there were ninety-six of us in all. One of the newcomers – Sergeant MILNE of the R.A.F. – was taken to the headquarters of the Kempei, kept there for a fortnight, as it was suspected he was connected with some underground movement in Batavia, and finally sent back to the stables. He told me that for the first three days there, he had been beaten up, and then left alone until he returned to the stables. One day just about this time the Korean guard on duty told us they had instructions to search for knives, as it was believed we were making knives in order to attack the guard. A search was made and the knives we had for cutting the bread taken from us. We were all taken out and lined up. The two guards then beat each of us up with the bamboo poles. I do not think the Japanese knew anything about this.

After ten months in the stables, we were finally moved

43

into the main camp and allowed to mix with the other prisoners. Conditions were much better there, and during our stay in the main camp there was no instance of ill-treatment. On 18th April 1945, we were taken from the camp at Batavia (Camp 1) to a camp at Bandoeng. This was an old Reform School made to house 400 boys. It now housed 3,000 prisoners of all Allied nationalities. On arrival, about 09.00 hours on the 19th April, 1945, our gear was searched and we were allowed into the camp compound, where we got soup and bread. We were then taken to a room. This room was about forty feet long by ten feet wide and round the walls there were three tiers of shelves on which the inmates slept. A Warrant-Officer told us that normally this would be accommodation for fourteen persons. Ninety-six of us occupied this room, the same number as occupied the stables in Batavia. There was very little water in this camp and we suffered more from the scarcity of water than from anything else during the time that we were there. It was so bad that if we wanted a drink at meal times, we had to drink the water in which we washed the dishes.

For about two months after our arrival, we worked from 09.00 hours until 18.00 hours, principally repairing houses which belonged to the Dutch, and were for the housing of Japanese officers. A Korean was running the camp. His name sounded like "KAZIAMA", and a Japanese Sergeant-Major whose name was "MORI" was in charge. Both men were of a brutal type and were notorious among the prisoners for their cruelty. One night, towards the end of this two months, there was a special parade of the whole camp, at which the Japanese asked for volunteers to repair aeroplane engines, ship's engines, and motor engines. About thirty volunteered from Dutch Army prisoners. No English-speaking prisoners came forward, and when the Japanese saw this, they sent for Wing Commander ALEXANDER, who was senior Allied Officer on this camp.

It appeared to us that they tried to get the Wing Commander to order us to do this work, but he refused.

Sergeant-Major "MORI" struck him and knocked him down. He broke ALEXANDER's jaw, and in all, knocked him down twelve times. The Wing Commander was then taken to hospital to be bandaged up, and Wing Commander NICHOLLS took over. "MORI", with a branch of a tree in his hand which had been given to him by "KAZIAMA", then walked round the ranks asking for volunteers, principally to repair bombers, and he particularly wanted some of the R.A.F. prisoners. When he saw that no one would volunteer, he called out all the senior ranks, including Wing Commander GRIGSON, Lieut. Commder THEW, Lieut Commder COOPER, Squadron Leader TAYLOR, Squadron Leader JARDINE, Lieut. Col. MAISIE, and Padre CHILDS of the R.A.F. "MORI" struck each one of them with his fists, and Squadron Leader JARDINE was knocked out. Then "KAZIAMA" went for GRIGSON and struck him on the side of the head with a branch of a tree. With the help of another Korean he knocked GRIGSON down, and kicked him repeatedly on the body with his boots. "MORI" then went to the officers' compound and without any warning struck Wing Commander MACGUIRE with a chair. He smashed the chair on the Wing Commander's back. Wing Commander NICHOLLS then spoke to "KAZIAMA" and told him that all we had was drivers. NICHOLLS then addressed us and told us that if we had to work for the Japanese, we should do all we could to hinder them rather than help them.

"KAZIAMA", who had been educated by some English missionaries in Korea, and who spoke perfect English, was standing by and heard all that was said by NICHOLLS. He let NICHOLLS speak and then several stepped forward from the ranks saying that they were drivers. "KAZIAMA" then sent for a Dutch Captain to see what knowledge they had of engines. This Captain questioned the volunteers and rejected some of them. We were then all allowed back to our quarters for supper. The time would be about 22.00 hours. The next morning we were paraded as usual at 07.30 hours and all went smoothly until dinner time. Another parade was called after dinner, about 14.00 hours. At this parade "KAZIAMA" was in charge and volunteers were asked for. This time the Japanese wanted Carpenters, Electricians, Plumbers, Blacksmiths, and almost every kind of craftsman, finishing up by again asking for drivers. A number of each class volunteered, and they were taken aside to be tested. From then onwards, and lasting for about a week, this sort of thing went on daily. Squadron Leader JARDINE was laid up for a week after the assault on him by "MORI". Finally it was a question of being detailed off in groups by the Japanese, whether or not we knew anything about the job on hand. About four hundred left the camp for Batavia, within a week or ten days of these parades.

I was one of a party supposed to be building a house for Sergeant-Major "MORI". I knew nothing about plumbing, nor in fact did any of the others, and we succeeded in wrecking about six houses in an attempt to build one decent one, which even after it had been more or less completed, only gave "MORI" shelter for about a week, as it began to fall to pieces and, needless to say the plumbing was terrible. "MORI" was then shifted back to the Japanese barracks at Bandoeng. Twice after that, when "MORI" met two prisoners from our lot he set about them. After we 'finished' the house, we were given the job as general caretakers and odd-job men at the Japanese Barracks in Bandoeng. I was chiefly engaged, along with six others, in repairing bicycles which the Japanese had stolen from the Dutch. From then until the war ended we were employed at the Barracks on jobs like these, and when we were not at the Barracks, we were given some job to do back at the camp. We were not subject to any further ill-treatment at the hands of the Japanese. We saw "MORI" and "KAZIAMA" almost every day, but they did not interfere with us.

There was one occasion when "KAZIAMA" beat up a Negro from the United States Merchant Navy because he believed he was gambling. On that occasion "MORI" interfered and sent the Negro back to his hut. "MORI" was about thirty years of age, five feet eight inches in height, very stout, dark hair and dark eyes, and he seemed to have a plentiful supply of teeth like most of the Japanese. "KAZIAMA" was much smaller in height and build. He would be about five feet three inches tall, was very slim, had fair hair, and was small featured. He was, of course, a Korean and did not appear to be more than twenty five years of age. "KAZIAMA", as I have said before, was apparently educated by British Missionaries in Korea, and he was fond of telling this to some of the prisoners. He spoke perfect English, but "MORI" only had a few words, mostly abuse which he had picked up from prisoners who called him "Bamboo MORI" because he used to strike them with bamboo poles.

About a fortnight before the war finished, about fifty prisoners from the camp at Bandoeng were taken in lorries from the camp on a four-hour trip up to the hills behind Bandoeng, and were set to work helping to make what looked like roads in some parts, and gun emplacements in others. We worked there from 10.00 hours until 17.00 hours daily, with the four-hour trip added on at each end of the day. The men were well treated, and the work on the hills seemed to be under the direction of the Japanese Army, members of which worked along with us. I was in this working party four times in all. One night after they had returned to camp, the following day's working party was cancelled. "MORI" and the Camp Commandant gave out the order. All the next day we just waited about in the camp, and all kinds of rumours went round, one of them being that the war was over. The following day we were visited by Lieut. Commander THEW, Captain of H.M.S. "JUPITER", and Senior Naval Officer in the camp, who told us that the Emperor of Japan had asked for an armistice, and had requested twelve days in which to get in touch with his troops. The twelve days had been granted. He also warned us to obey implicitly any order given by our own officers, as the Japanese were still armed and could do what they liked until our troops would arrive in Java.

We were told to keep this information to ourselves, and on no account to let the Japanese know that we had any of this information. Two days later, all British, American and Indian prisoners were transferred to the camp at Batavia (Camp 1). It was obvious, when we arrived there, that a great change had taken place. Roll call was taken by our own officers and the day after we arrived, Lieut. FORBES, formally of the "STRONGHOLD" who was acting as Camp Adjutant, called us together and read out to us a letter which had been received from Colonel KAWABE, the Japanese Officer in command of all prison camps. This letter informed us that we had won the war, and that Colonel KAWABE was waiting instructions from the Commander-in-Chief, South East Asia Command. From then onwards we received plenty of food, fruit, clothing and medical supplies and it was six weeks later before H.M.S. "CUMBERLAND" arrived with Admiral PATTERSON on board. We stayed a further week in the camp and then were taken – naval ranks only, to Singapore, where we arrived three days later. The Army and Air Force prisoners followed in a Japanese troopship. We made the journey home on the Anchor Liner "CILICIA" and arrived in Liverpool on the 29th of October 1945.

During the time I was a prisoner, I was able to find out a little more about the six-inch cruiser which had sunk the "BEHAR". The first thing was that this vessel carried three seaplanes and they each bore the number "102". The ship carried no guns aft, but had four torpedo tubes on either side. She was about the same size as H.M.S. "EXETER". Captain GREEN, when we were leaving the ship, asked me how many funnels she had, and I replied that I thought she had one. He told me to look again, and I saw that the ship had really two small funnels which joined together as one at the top. Again on reaching Batavia, it appears that the Indian members of our crew were put to work getting rice and vegetables on board this cruiser, and taking empty boxes and bags from her into a barge. Every item of stores being put aboard her was marked "102". When the six-inch cruiser had finished loading, the barge was towed alongside the eight-inch cruiser. At that time there were some stores in *the barge marked "104", which the Indians were not allowed to handle. The conclusion was that the number "102" signified the six-inch cruiser, while "104" appeared to denote the eight-inch cruiser. The latter had two twin turrets forward and one aft. Both cruisers appeared to have been painted black, but their general appearance was that they had not been in dry-dock since the war had started for they were rusty and dirty looking.'*

The Korean KAZIAMA and the Japanese Sergeant "Bamboo" MORI mentioned by Macleod at Bandoeng POW camp were two well known notorious characters, who had ill treated prisoners elsewhere in the Far East, being at Haruku in the Moluccas for the construction by allied POWs of an airfield. Of over 2,300 prisoners sent there, only about 700 survived. Kaziama and Mori were on the hellship "Maros Maru" with 500 Dutch and British POWs plus others picked up from another sunken Japanese vessel, which took 127 days to reach Sourabaya from Ambon. Fewer than one in two prisoners survived the voyage. "Bamboo" MORI was tried for War Crimes and was duly hanged after the war. KAZIAMA (Kasayama) received life imprisonment, but it seems doubtful that he finished the sentence, as most war criminals were released by the Japanese during the 1950s.

Mr Phillips, the Chief Officer of the "BEHAR", following his repatriation gave a detailed account of his experiences to Captain J. Chrisopher, the Hain Steamship Company's marine superintendent at Cardiff on 31st October 1945, which was passed on as a memo dated 1st November signed by Captain Christopher to the head office in London. The following extract of the "memo" relates to the story given by Mr Phillips following completion of his interrogation by the Japanese in Batavia:

'On April 28th this whole party was returned to Naval Barracks where was found that twenty Indian members of BEHAR's crew had been landed from cruiser "102"

and were housed in the barracks. Mr Phillips has no information whatever concerning the 69 members of BEHAR's crew that remained aboard cruiser "102".

The two female passengers did not return to the Barracks until May 1st which date the whole party was photographed. Food during this second period at Barracks was similar to the previous ration, consisting of 3 small quantities of boiled rice and spoonful of raw cabbage each day.

On May 21st the party was again split up and the following were taken to Prisoner of War Camp No.1 Batavia, Java:-

Mr Phillips, Mr Weir, P.O. Griffiths, A.Bs. Macleod and Kershaw, Flt.Sergt. Barr and Dr.Lee.

The remainder were retained at the Barracks, with the exception of Mrs. Shaw and Mrs. Pascovi, who were removed to the Civil Internment Camp on the island.

At the Prisoner of War Camp, the party were put into a dark cell, where 18 members of the crew were already confined, the whole party being kept therein for two days and nights. It was only after the joining up of these two parties that Mr. Phillips learned that two Indian members of the crew had died since landing through malnutrition, dysentery, etc., and an absolute absence of medical attention. From there the party was removed to the isolation part of the camp and housed in an old cavalry stable where it remained immured for ten weary months.

Mr. Phillips describes this period as being one of intense mental and physical torture, corporal punishment being, to most of the party, a daily occurrence. Food rations were of very meagre proportions and extremely poor quality, exercise practically non-existent and any means of recreation or relaxation just not to hand. The guards, apparently quite free of any semblance of discipline, took obvious and malicious pleasure in inflicting punishment and insult. The quarters were much overcrowded, mats, on the cement floor the only mattresses provided, no other covering being issued. Conditions were verminous, dysentery, malaria and dengue fever, beriberi and other tropical diseases were very prevalent and medical attention at times non-existent, and always difficult to obtain. One deck serang, Hossein Belal, died of dysentery 27.5.44. The unfortunate occupants of this black hole rose from 23 in number to 94 before removal to the main camp and despite all the continuous efforts of the British Camp Commandant, Wing Commander Alexander, to improve the conditions prevailing, such persisted right through.

On March 18th 1945 the whole of the occupants of this stable were removed to the main prisoner of war camp, where they were allowed to mix freely with other prisoners. Up to this date the punishment for attempted intercourse between their party and other prisoners was death.

Once in the main camp the party came under the administration of the British Camp Commander and his staff, and conditions were somewhat improved; members were free to join working parties, etc., which helped towards relieving the deadly monotony, besides giving them 10 cents per day, which allowed of the purchase of small quantities of fruit and tobacco.

During the whole of Mr. Phillips's incarceration only one issue of Red Cross Parcels was made.

On June 18th 1945 Mr. Phillip's party was removed to a Prisoner of War Camp at Bandoeng, where the climatic conditions were intensely cold, no extra clothing of any description being issued. The camp itself was originally a boys' reformatory built to house some 400. It now held upwards of 4,000 prisoners of war and work was actually going forward to increase the housing by a further 2,000. Conditions here were definitely worse than before, sleeping accommodation being arranged in three tiers of wooden shelves, with sleepers lying shoulder to shoulder with no room to even turn. The lavatory accommodation was unbelievably inadequate, the water supply even worse. The bread supplied was made of tapioca flour, unleavened, with a consistency of gutta percha and almost indigestible. The daily meat ration consisted of the entrails only of one bullock between 4,000 men, once per week. *Corporal punishment increased in frequency and brutality considerably and after repeated refusals on the part of prisoners to work on aero engine repairs., Mr. Phillips affirms that conditions generally became bestial. These conditions persisted right through to the cessation of hostilities, when we understand that the Jap authorities fell over themselves in attempts to ingratiate themselves with the prisoners. In addition to large increase of foodstuffs, medical supplies of obvious British origin were issued, in many cases too late to save the lives and reasons of thousands of prisoners. Such supplies had obviously been in Japanese hands long before they were actually issued.*

On August 24th 1945 all the British prisoners were removed back to Batavia being housed in the original camp, until liberation by the R.A.P.W.I. on September 24th.

We have been given a further recommendation of Seacunny Gafoor Goodal. Mr. Phillips, who reports that this rating proved himself to be a tower of strength to him during a most trying time. This seacunny, in addition to speaking quite excellent English, soon picked up the Japanese language and was thus able to assist Mr. Phillips very materially in his handling of the Indian members of the crew, passing on guards' orders, etc. He was at all times cheerful, optimistic, and his disposition went a long way in helping to preserve discipline and cheerfulness in their own small party. Mr. Phillips states that he afterwards learned that during a period that he himself, was delirious with malaria and dysentery, Gafoor Goodal fed him with the more palatable portions of his own meagre rations, in addition to running grave risks of serious punishment through stealing fruit, etc., from the Japanese guards, with same end in view.

The foregoing is a very bare outline of the suffering that these men of ours have undergone, but we have been told enough to marvel at the fortitude they have displayed, and the fact that they look as well as they do'.

Following liberation Mr Phillips was taken aboard HMS

CUMBERLAND, where he was de-briefed concerning what had happened to the "BEHAR", the time spent on the cruiser "TONE" although of course at this stage he had no knowledge of the cruiser's name, except to identify it as cruiser "102". He also gave the information that 68 crew and 1 passenger were last seen aboard the cruiser on the 16th March 1944. Petty Officer Griffiths went down to the women's camp following the surrender, and was able to establish that the two passengers Mrs Shaw and Mrs Pascheove were still alive. 17 Indian (and Goanese) ratings survived captivity in Java. Captain Symons, Radio Officer Walker, Captain Green, and the three New Zealand naval officers, Benge, Godwin, and Parker all survived their harsh and inhuman treatment in Japan.

Mr Phillips arrived at Cardiff railway station, and had to make his own way home by tram, his family unaware that he was coming. The experiences of his treatment, and those meted out to his shipmates by the Japanese were to mentally scar him for life. An engineer who was to sail with him in 1956 aboard the S.S. TREGOTHNAN informed the author "I remember Captain Phillips as a quiet brooding man and in the wardroom given to long silences. He smoked holding his cigarette between his index finger and thumb in the Oriental style. He never spoke of his war service".

Lloyd's "War Loss Card" regarding the "BEHAR" reports that in January 1945 the ship's owners were informed by the Master's wife that he is reported to have broadcast twice from Tokyo. A.R. Walker, Chief Radio Officer broadcast from Tokyo December 19 1944. The reason for these radio broadcasts is not clear, but it is known the Japanese did use prisoners on a number of occasions to make broadcasts. Perhaps by this stage of the war, with it going so badly for Japan, they realised there would be a day of reckoning coming, and wanted to give the impression that prisoners were alive and well, or the exact opposite – that it was a note of defiance, letting the Allies know that Japanese shipping was getting through to Japan from other parts of the Far East, and that her ships were carrying prisoners, which once that became known would stop the Allies from attacking them, for fear of killing Allied prisoners. However if this latter theory was their aim, they were very much mistaken in the influence it would have on Allied strategy.

On 12th September 1944 the "RAKUYO MARU" and the "KACHIDOKI MARU" were sunk by two American submarines in the South China Sea with huge loss of life, although at that time the submarines had no knowledge that the ships were carrying POW's. It was only in the late afternoon of the 15th that the American submarine "PAMPANITO" found survivors in the water, and both her and another American submarine "SEALION" rescued as many survivors as they could find. Miraculously on the 17th September five days after the sinkings, the American submarine "BARB" found 14 more survivors and rescued them. These were the first Allied prisoners who had worked on the infamous "Burma-Siam Railway" to be recovered by the Allies, their rescue being kept secret for quite sometime. However the knowledge that the Japanese were shipping large numbers of prisoners to Japan did not deter the Allies from sinking any Japanese ships that were located by submarines or aircraft after the sinking of the above two ships. On November 17th 1944 the Australian Government made public the story of the sinkings and the recovery of British and Australian POW's and the atrocities committed by the Japanese on the "Death Railway". Perhaps this revelation to the world had some bearing on the decision to use POW's for propaganda broadcasts by the Japanese.

Sources of information.

PRO KEW files WO311/564 235/1089 311/562 311/549
Registry of Shipping & Seaman, Cardiff
Guildhall Library, London "Lloyd's shipping collection".
U.S. Navy Archives.

NOTES

Time zones.
During the war Japanese occupied territory kept Tokyo time which is 9 hours ahead of GMT.
Normally Sumatra and Java would have been 7 hours ahead of GMT.

RAPWI
Recovery of Allied Prisoners of War and Internees.

THE IDENTIFICATION OF "CRUISER 102" AND JAPANESE NAVAL PERSONNEL INVOLVED.

When RAPWI (Recovery of Allied Prisoners of War and Internees) party rescued the prisoners, which in the case of the "BEHAR" survivors held in Java, was on 24th September 1945, it obviously would have been told that other prisoners from the ship were last seen on the Japanese cruiser "102". Once RAPWI had documented all the prisoners rescued in the Far East, it would become apparent that there was a large number of prisoners from the "BEHAR" unaccounted for. The first step being to trace the identity of cruiser "102", and what became of that vessel. Although Japan suffered severe naval losses at sea, cruiser "102" (TONE) had been bombed and sunk in shallow water near Kure in position 34.14N 132.27E. on 24th July 1945. Whilst on 28th July cruiser "104", the "AOBA", was sunk in Kure Naval Dockyard after being bombed by American aircraft after partially being damaged in an air attack the same day as the sinking of the "TONE".

Following the occupation of Japan, the American Naval Intelligence were very thorough in their investigations, and confiscated all military documents belonging to the enemy they found anywhere, which they considered of importance. In the case of the "TONE" being fortunate to find the log of the cruiser, and by 16th January 1946 had passed on to the British Admiralty Delegation in Washington the identity of the vessel that had sunk the "BEHAR", who informed the Director of Naval Intelligence Admiralty in the following communication.

Source PRO KEW WO 311/564

British Naval Staff
Combined Chiefs of Staff
Bldg.,
Washington D.C.

BRITISH ADMIRALTY DELEGATION
RESTRICTED

From   C.O.I.S.B.A.D. Washington
To   Director of Naval Intelligence Admiralty

Copy to B.N.L.O.S.C.A.P.Tokyo
S.O.(I) E.I. Colombo
C.O.I.S.B.P.F.Hong Kong

Date 16th January, 1946.   Ref. 19-1

Captured document now available at OP-23F141/S. Office of Naval Intelligence, Washington reveals that the S.S. BEHAR was sunk by Japanese Heavy Cruiser TONE. The report states that all survivors were picked up and that the TONE thereafter proceeded to Jakarta and remained in the Singapore-Linga area. It is not stated what disposal was made of the prisoners picked up from the S.S. BEHAR. TONE log further reveals that S.S.BEHAR was sunk in position 087.00 East 20.34 South, at 091553 March 1944.

2. The above information is supplied in the hope that authorities having knowledge of heavy cruiser TONE's detailed movements can be contacted with a view to solving the problem of the missing men.

Sgd. H.R.M.LAIRD
Captain R.N.

The hunt was now on for the Captain of the "TONE" to discover what had become of the prisoners left on this vessel on the 16th of March 1944. In this the British authorities were successful, and by 5th March 1946 a secret signal addressed to the Admiralty gave the following details;

Source PRO KEW WO 311/564

SECRET

From UKNA (United Kingdom Liasion Mission Tokyo)
Date 5.3.46
Time 0812

Addressed   Admiralty

Info   C.O.I.S. Britpacflt,
S.O.I. East Indies
C.O.I.S.B.A.D. Washington

IMPORTANT
MY 020355.

1.   Captain of TONE has admitted

(a) Fifteen survivors of BEHAR including two white women were landed in Batavia.

(b) All remaining survivors were killed on board TONE.

(c) Killing was in accordance with operation orders issued by Admiral Takasu C. in C. South West Area Fleet who is dead.

(d) Executive order for killing was given by Vice Admiral Sakonju repetition Sakonju Commanding Japanese 16 Squadron.

2.   Appropriate action is being taken in regard
            to all personnel involved. Request no
            repetition no publicity while investigation is
            in progress

                                              050812Z

The need for secrecy was essential in order not to
pre-warn the Japanese concerned with the "BEHAR"
executions that the Allied war crimes branch were
looking for them. The Hain Steamship Company was
requested not to publicly print anything about the loss of
the "BEHAR" and this ban was passed by Hains to
Lloyds. In the meantime, survivors of the "BEHAR" were
approached by the Judge Advocate General's
department of the War Office, to make affidavits
concerning their experiences and events they witnessed.
Curiously no affidavits appear to have been made by the
ship's officers, with the exception of the Chief Radio
Officer, who made a sworn statement concerning ill-
treatment on the "SANUKI MARU", during the passage
that he and the five others made from Java to Japan via
Singapore, but this affidavit was not relevant to the
investigations concerning the missing survivors and the
subsequent trial which followed.
The investigations were carried out in Tokyo, but by
August 1946, there appeared a difference of opinion by
various parties concerned on where the trial should be
held. ALFSEA wanting the trial in Hong Kong as the ship
and civilians were all British, whilst the UK Naval Adviser
and British War Crimes Tokyo wanted the trial to be in
Japan. ALFSEA sent a cipher telegram on 23rd August
to the British Minor War Crimes Tokyo with Information
copied to the War Office and UKLIM Land Forces Hong
Kong, which agreed to the continued investigation in
Japan, but when completed, suggested the accused to
be shipped to Hong Kong as soon as possible, if the
Royal Navy agree, by destroyer. The telegram requested
Admiralty views. The preferred view was Hong Kong.
Originally the trial of the accused in the "BEHAR" affair

was to start in February 1947, but was delayed until September of that year. In a cipher telegram from the British War Crimes Investigation team, Tokyo Office, to the War Office, London dated 21st January 1947, it stated that the "BEHAR" case had been fully investigated and that ten persons had been accused, of these two were dead, one had absconded, and the remainder arrested.

The abstract of evidence in the case of Rear Admiral Sakonju Naomasa and Mayuzumi Haruo prepared by the prosecution now follows in full;

Source PRO KEW WO 311/564

'ABSTRACT OF EVIDENCE IN THE CASE OF REAR ADMIRAL SAKONJU NAOMASA AND CAPTAIN MAYAZUMI HARUO.

During February 1944, the Japanese South West Area Fleet under command of Admiral Takasu, now deceased, planned an operation in the Indian Ocean for the disruption of Allied lines of communication, and for the capture of Allied shipping.

The Japanese 16th Squadron under command of Vice-Admiral SAKONJU Naomasa, whose Chief of Staff was Captain SHIMANOUCHI Momochiyo was ordered to carry out the operation and the following ships took part; heavy cruisers "Aoba" carrying the flag of Vice Admiral SAKONJU Naomasa, "Chikuma" and "Tone"; the light cruisers "Kinu", "Oi", three destroyers and three or four submarines supported by an air force.

Before the operation was carried out emphasis was laid on the secrecy that must be maintained, at a conference held at Penang on February 23rd 1944, and in connection with this Secrecy was the suggestion that should a ship be captured and/or sunk, only prisoners essential for the giving of information were to be brought back, the remainder were to be executed.

The operation opened on February 28th 1944, after all ships were fully ammunitioned, victualled and fuelled and at about 1100 hours on March 9th 1944, the "Tone" reported sighting a merchant vessel which was the British M.V. "BEHAR". The "Tone" ordered her to stop and opened fire which resulted in the sinking of the "Behar", the latter vessel not replying to the firing of the Japanese cruiser.

After the sinking, survivors numbering not less than eighty were taken on board the cruiser "Tone". They were later taken below decks and transported to Batavia, the H.Q. of the South West Area Fleet, where a number of "essential persons" were taken ashore and lodged in camps. The remainder, estimated at about 65, were kept on board the "Tone" which was then detached from the squadron and left to join her original command, the 7th Squadron at Linga. On the way these survivors were executed about midnight on the night of 18/19th March, on the quarter-deck of the "Tone" on the direct orders of Captain MAYAZUMI.

P.J. GREENE in person, and J.G. GODWIN, C.O.H. KERSHAW and W.L. GRIFFITHS by affidavit, will testify to the fact that they were passengers on the M.V. "BEHAR", and that the vessel was sunk by the Japanese cruiser "Tone", and they, with the remainder of the ship's crew and officers were taken to Batavia as such on the "Tone". That they were called out from amongst the prisoners along with eleven other survivors and they were taken off the "Tone", and aboard the "Aoba" and later to camps on the mainland at Batavia; and that the remaining survivors were kept on board the "Tone".

MII JUNSUKE, who was an officer on board the "Tone" under command of Captain MAYAZUMI will testify that he saw survivors from the "Behar" tied with rope on the quarter-deck of the "Tone" when they were awaiting interrogation, and that the "Tone" signalled the number of prisoners on board and requested permission to land them at Batavia and that this request was refused and orders sent back for the DISPOSAL of the survivors; that the word "DISPOSAL" meant "put to death"; that the Captain of the "Tone" repeated attempts to get the prisoners taken off the "Tone" and placed in camps, and

60

that his efforts failed; and that the execution was carried out on board the "Tone" after she had left Batavia on the way to join her original command, the 7th Squadron.

NAGAI KUNIO, who was the Chief Paymaster on board the "TONE" will testify that he was the interpreter at the interrogation of the survivors and that no list of them was taken; that the execution took place on the "TONE" between Batavia and LINGA and that Lieut. ISHIWARA performed the execution on direct orders from CAPT. MAYAZUMI.

SHIMANOUCHI MOMOCHIYO, who was Senior Staff Officer of the 16th Squadron will testify that the Operational Order issued by Admiral TAKASU, was not signed by him but was accepted as an order of his; that there was no mention of DISPOSAL of Prisoners in the Operational Order (Issued by Admiral TAKASU); that at the conference held at Fleet H.Q.; Admiral TAKASU stated that essential prisoners would be brought back; that his own statement should read on translation "Minimum number of prisoners essential for information only should be brought back". That this order was a verbal order from Admiral TAKASU; that Admiral SAKONJU signalled the "TONE" – "Keep only the minimum of prisoners and dispose of the rest; that the word "DISPOSE" meant execute; that the Captain of the "TONE" repeatedly applied to Admiral SAKONJU for permission to take all prisoners to Batavia and his requests were refused; that Admiral SAKONJU ordered the Captain of the "TONE" (at Batavia), to land essential prisoners and the remainder were to be disposed of. That the "TONE" was no longer under the command of the 16th Squadron when she sailed for Linga and would be under the command of the 7th Squadron; but that the 7th Squadron have had nothing to do with the execution; that a memorandum stating the method used to execute the prisoners was seen by him at Singapore three months after the event.

The prosecution will produce sworn voluntary statements made by each of the Accused.

Authors note.
C.O.H. Kershaw and W.L. Griffiths were not passengers but Royal Navy DEMS personnel.

The following undated letter, and un-addressed letter exists in PRO Files at KEW and can reasonably be deducted that it was sent in 1947 possibly addressed to the WAR OFFICE, or the ADMIRALTY and ended up in the Judge Advocate General's Office of the WAR OFFICE. It is of significance in that it shows the desire of Captain Green to attend the War Crimes trial, and assist in the proper course of justice.

17 Bench Street,
Dover.

Dear Sir,
I am an ex P.O.W. Japan, survivor of M.V. "BEHAR" sunk 9th March 1944 by the Japanese cruiser "TONI".

I hear that certain senior officers of this Cruiser have been arrested for the murder of 72 of the crew. Your information about this incident may be complete, but I also have certain details which may be of use to you in connection with this.

Shortly after being sunk and taken aboard as a prisoner this vessel was joined by another cruiser of the same class and a light Cruiser of approximately 5,000 – 6000 tons with 6" guns and torpedo armament.

It was the practice of these vessels to occasionally leave the line, but they always returned before sundown, when they always adopted a 90° evasive turn.

Two or three days after my capture I had the opportunity of viewing the horizon and saw a huge column of smoke which in my opinion was probably a tanker caught by one of the cruisers.

I regret that I am unable to give any information of possible survivors.

On arrival at Batavia, fifteen of us were detached from the rest and sent aboard this light Cruiser for two days before being transferred ashore. This ship was flying an Admirals flag and it must have been with his consent that the mass murder took place aboard the "TONI". I do not doubt that every effort will be made, on the part of the proper authority to arrest and sentence this Admiral who was undoubtedly fully responsible in this mass murder.

I am returning to China in 6 – 8 weeks time and should be pleased to volunteer, in any capacity if needed, to assist in the proper course of justice. If proved guilty I desire, if possible to assist in his or their final despatch as an act of retribution for my shipmates who were the victims.

Yours faithfully,
Capt. P.J. Green

CHARGE SHEET

The accused;-

Rear Admiral   SAKONJU Naomasa
Captain   MAYAZUMI Haruo

of the Imperial Japanese Navy

attached to are charged with

COMMITTING A WAR CRIME
in that

on the High Seas at or about midnight on the 18/19th March 1944, the accused Rear Admiral SAKONJU Naomasa as Commanding Officer of the 16th Squadron, South-West area Fleet, and accused Captain MAYAZUMI Haruo, as officer-in-command of H.I.J.M.S. "TONE", were in violation of the laws and usages of war, together concerned in the killing of approximately sixty-five survivors from the sinking of the British M.V. "BEHAR", being members of the crew or passengers on the said vessel.

Singapore
1947

Commanding

....
(Signature of Convening Officer)

Singapore
1947

Major-General,
Commanding Singapore District.

Sources of Information

PRO KEW file WO 311/564

One interesting aspect of the trial is why did the "Charge Sheet" accuse the Japanese with the approximate killing of 65 survivors, when before the trial commenced it was known that the figure was 69? Originally the trial was to have taken place in February

1947, but was postponed for some still unknown reason, but even by February 1947 the figure of 69 was established.

It must have been known by the owners of the ship in 1946 the number of crew aboard the "BEHAR" was 98 including the "DEMS" personnel signed on as "Deckhands". The shipowner would also have known from its agents how many passengers were embarked in New Zealand and Australia. From the survivors who did return, it would have been discovered, the names of those that died in the action leading to the sinking of the vessel, those who died in captivity, and passenger who was taken away by the Japanese whilst in captivity, and never seen again. Thus leaving a balance of 69 persons to be accounted for.

By February 1947 the exact number of "BEHAR" survivors left on board the "TONE" on March 16th 1944 was known both by the Hain Steamship Company, and the Judge Advocate General's Office in London, this is proven by the fact that a letter dated 3rd February 1947 from the latter office to Mr. Angus Macleod in Stornoway, under the title "Sinking of MV "BEHAR" and Alleged Massacre of 69 Survivors thereof." The letter contained photographs of alleged Japanese concerned with the incident, and asking if Mr Macleod can identify any of the men who participated in any ill-treatment of survivors". The letter from the Hain Steamship Company dated 8th March 1947, to the Judge Advocate General's Office has the same heading with the additional prefix of "Japanese War Crimes" and concerns the fate of the 3rd Radio Officer Gordon Henry Cumming, whose father had been making strenuous efforts to discover the fate of his son, who had not returned home after the war ended.

Author's note.
There is confusion in the correct spelling of the name of the Captain of the "TONE". On the 12th March 1947 he made two affidavits where his name is given on one document as "MAYAZUMI" whilst on the other it is given as "MAYUZUMI", this latter spelling is also given on an

affidavit dated 17th March 1947. On the Charge Sheet, the spelling used is "MAYAZUMI".

There is confusion over the rank of Sakonju Naomasa, the charge sheet has his rank as Rear-Admiral, whilst his affidavit submitted at the trial, records the rank as Vice-Admiral.

After the trial, information released to the news agencies concerning the outcome, referred to the accused as Rear-Admiral Sakonju and Captain Mayazumi.

TRIAL INFORMATION

WAR CRIMES TRIAL HONG KONG   Case No 65278
Held at Jardine Matheson's East Point Godown

TRIAL COMMENCED 19TH SEPTEMBER 1947 at 1000
hours. ENDED 29TH OCTOBER 1947

SWORN AFFIDAVITS FROM SURVIVORS USED IN
TRIAL.

W.L. GRIFFITHS	Petty officer I/C DEMS PERSONNEL
C.P.J. KERSHAW	AB ASDIC OPERATOR
A.MACLEOD	AB. ASIDIC OPERATOR
CAPTAIN P.J. GREEN	Merchant Service Captain sailing as passenger
LT.S.C.PARKER	RNZNVR sailing as passenger
SUB.LT. J.G. GODWIN	RNZNVR sailing as passenger

CAPTAIN P.J. GREEN attended war crimes trial and
gave evidence on 25th and 26th September 1947.

SWORN AFFIDAVITS FROM JAPANESE
USED IN TRIAL.

Vice Admiral Sakonju Naomasa
             Cmdr 16th Squadron SW area Pacific
             Fleet.

Captain Mayazumi Haruo
             Captain of Imperial Japanese Navy
             Cruiser TONE

Source of Information: PRO KEW WO 235/1089

Background information.

15th March 1944   "TONE" arrived Tandjong Priok about 1 hour before sunset.

16th March 1944   15 Europeans including Chinese Doctor transferred to Japanese cruiser "AOBA".

18th March 1944   15 Europeans landed Tandjong Priok from "AOBA" and taken to Batavia. 2 0 Indian Crew landed Tandjong Priok from cruiser "TONE".

Between 1700 and 1800 hours local time 18th March 1944 "TONE" sailed for Singapore via the Bangka Strait, it was previously decided that the executions would take place about 40 to 50 miles from Batavia before reaching the strait. At 2200 hours TOKYO time, 3 hours before reaching Bangka Strait, Captain Mayazumi instructed Lt. Ishihara to carry out the executions. Just before entering Bangka Strait, Lt. Ishihara reported that the executions had been carried out. Commander Mii refused to be associated with the executions, and the order to execute the prisoners from Captain Mayazumi passed direct to Lt. Ishihara Takonari.

Other known officers taking part in executions.
Lieut. Tani
Sub. Lt. Tanaka
Sub Lt, Otsuka
Sub Lt. Kinoshita*
Sub Lt. Yoshioka*

* In a sworn statement 17.3.47 made by Captain Mayazumi both these officers were stated to be dead.

Lt. ISHIHARA Takonari who was in charge of the execution party was seen early March or the end of February 1946 by Captain Mayazumi at the Second Demobilisation Ministry Tokyo, when he was called in for interrogation with regard to the "BEHAR" case. Ishihara was living in a room within the Ministry whilst he was being interrogated. However he did not appear before Military trial held in Hong Kong. The suspicion being that he absconded in Japan after the interrogation. However he was in custody in 1949 when he made a sworn affidavit concerning the executions.

Authors note.
Although the date officially given for the executions is the 18/19th March, the factual date must have been the 18th March 1944, as the executions started at 2200 Tokyo time i.e. 1300 GMT on 18th and were completed within 3 hours when the vessel entered Bangka Strait.

The affidavit by Rear Admiral SAKONJU Naomasa is given in full:
I Capt.E.C. Watson certify that I have now fully warned the accused, Sakonju Naomasa in the following terms :–

"Do you wish to make a statement or to give evidence on oath? You are not obliged to say anything or give evidence unless you wish to do so, but whatever you say or any evidence you give will be taken down in writing, and may be given in evidence". R.P. (4) E.

The accused, Sakonju Naomasa states he will make a statement upon oath.

Signature E.C.Watson Capt.
Date 16.4.47.

I, Sakonju Naomasa make oath and say as follows :–

I have been fully warned that I am not obliged to make any statement, but that whatever I say will be taken down in writing and may be used in evidence. I wish to state voluntarily that, my full name is Sakonju Naomasa, I held the rank of Vice-Admiral and Chief of Staff of the Japanese – China Seas Fleet.

Early in 1944, I was the Commanding Officer of the 16th Squadron. My flag ship was the "Ashigara" and later my flag was changed to the "Aoba", based at Singapore. About the end of February or the beginning of March of that year an order was issued for an operation in the Indian Ocean. This order was issued by Vice Admiral Takasu Shiro, Commander in Chief of the South West Area Fleet. The order contained the disruption of Allied communications in the Indian Ocean.

At first Vice Admiral Takasu was at Penang and the detailed order was worked out at his H.Q. One of my officers, Commander Shimanouchi, was called to Penang for the conference.

Later Vice Admiral Takasu's H.Q. were transferred to Sourabaya and Lt. Commander Koyamada, one of my Staff Officers, was sent there to discuss the operational plans and the detailed plan was completed at end of February. The Capture of shipping was the primary purpose of the plan. In the written order the sinking of vessels was not mentioned but if the Allied shipping tried to escape it was judged necessary to sink them.

Some of the orders were not included in the original order and an additional order specifying details was issued to the 16th Squadron.

The order was issued to the light cruisers, "Kinu" and "Oi" and the destroyers "Shikimami", "Uranami", and "Amargiri", also the three heavy cruisers "Tone", "Chikuma", and "Aoba". In the operation an air force attached to the South West Area Fleet was co-operated although an air force was not under my jurisdiction.

The disposal of prisoners of war was specified in the operational order issued by the South West Area Fleet Headquarters.

I, as Commander of the 16th Squadron accepted the order and in turn an order to the same effect was issued by me to the 16th Squadron. The details of the order were as follows:

In the first part of February, according to my memory, Staff Officer SHIMANOUCHI of the 16th Squadron returned to my flag ship "Aoba", which was at the time at SINGAPORE, from PENANG, where he had attended the conference of the South West Area Fleet Headquarters to discuss an operational plan for that particular campaign.

I asked KOYAMADA the policy of the Headquarters in regard to the disposal of prisoners of war and he replied "In view of the fact that the Allies are lately killing Japanese prisoners of war at GUADALCANAL by running tanks over them and are often bombing and torpedoing Japanese hospital ships, causing many casualties, the H.Q. came to a conclusion that the Allies are aiming at the reduction of Japan's man power, and H.Q. decided to retaliate." I said "Is that so!" I decided to accept the order to dispose of prisoner's of war. During the proceeding month, that is January, the light cruisers "KUMA" and "KITAGAMI" were sunk and heavily damaged by the enemy submarine action and many of my men were lost. The spirit of retaliation in fair combat was running high at that time among the officers and men of the 16th Squadron.

As to the order for the disposal of the prisoners of war, I hold myself responsible, although such an order was given to me by the South West Area Fleet Commander. At the time the Chief of Staff of the South West Area Fleet was Vice Admiral TADA and the Assistant Chief of Staff was Rear Admiral NISHIO, they must have read the order covering every detail of the Operational Plan and detailed orders of the 16th Squadron were also sent to them. Neither of these officers issued any order or instructions to suspend the disposal order. When the "TONE" sank the "BEHAR" and took on board survivors, I know that the Captain of the "TONE" contacted the "AOBA" and gave information but did not ask for instructions as to the disposal of the survivors.

I signalled, the "TONE" was to dispose of the P.O.Ws. as previously ordered, I knew there were women among the survivors but I did not know how many there were at the time I replied to the signal from the "TONE". I learned that the order for execution had not been carried out at

Batavia from Staff Officer Koyamada. On arrival at BATAVIA the Captain of the "TONE" did not report to me what action he had taken and shortly afterwards the 16th Squadron disbanded and the "TONE" and "CHIKUMA", which had been temporarily attached to the 16th Squadron for the operation left the Squadron and I never knew what was done to the survivors. I don't remember whether 16 Europeans were sent to the "AOBA" but I recall that some of the survivors were subjected to reinterrogation.

Immediately I arrived in Batavia I went ashore and do not know what happened to the survivors that were still on board the "TONE". I presumed all survivors were sent to Batavia or SOURABAYA where the Headquarters of the South West Area Fleet was located and some of the survivors were removed from the "TONE" to the "AOBA" then to SOURABAYA as both vessels left within a few days.

The day after we reached Batavia, which I remember was about March 14 or thereabouts, a conference was held aboard the cruiser "AOBA" to review the operation that had just been completed in the Indian Ocean. Commander SUGIE a Staff Officer of the South West Area Fleet was present. The conference lasted for half a day and during that day the 16th Squadron was discontinued taking "TONE" and the "CHIKUMA" from my command, the Captain of the "TONE" made no report to me concerning the disposal of the survivors but I knew his failure to carry out the command and I did not press the matter further.

I do not know whether Captain of the "TONE" sent any of the Indian members of the crew of the "BEHAR" ashore in Batavia but they may have been so dealt with after I left the ship to stay ashore in Batavia. I received no report of the execution of the survivors of the "BEHAR" on board the "TONE" on the night of March 18th, the "TONE" was no longer under my command. I presume that the Captain of the "TONE" tried to hand the survivors over to the prisoners of war camp in Batavia and I believe that he executed them possibly because he had been so requested to do by the prisoners of war camp authorities or possibly in accordance with my previous order with regard to this operation although he was no longer under my command, and did not realise this.

I was of the opinion that the disposal of the prisoners of war was ordered for that particular campaign but that the order had not been carried out. As far as I know the order for the disposal of the prisoners of war was issued by the South West Area Fleet Command and higher authorities had nothing to do with it. I knew nothing of a general order of this type being issued to the Japanese Navy. The Japanese Naval and Military authorities at that time believed that the Allied aim was to destroy Japan's man power so it was favoured by them to do the same to the Allies. The Japanese Army adopted a slogan "One Japanese soldier should kill at least ten Allied men when he makes a suicide attack", but there was no order specifying that the Allied survivors were to be disposed of. Japanese Naval officers and men knew that they should refrain from any violation of the International Law and although they did not memorise the KAISEN HOKI (Rules of Naval Warfare) but they knew that prisoners of war and survivors of ships sunk should be protected and saved from violence. The order that was passed to the "TONE" was not included in the rules contained in the Rules for Naval Warfare, but at the time sentiment among a few of the Japanese commanders favoured the execution of the survivors of ships sunk, on the ground that reports had been received concerning the Japanese prisoners of war being run over and killed by tanks in the GUADALCANAL, and Japanese hospital ships being attacked indicating that the Allies were contravening the International Law. I did not have frequent contact with the high authorities ashore and so I cannot say whether this sentiment was shared by them. I cannot say whether Admiral TAKASU issued the order on his own responsibility or not. I would say that the Captain of the "TONE" and all other officers and men on that ship were not responsible as they carried out an order given to them. I believe that Admiral TAKASU and myself should take the full responsibility, if the execution had been carried out whilst the "TONE" was under my command.

(signed) Sakonju Naomasa

The following affidavit made on 12th March 1947 by the Captain of the "TONE".

I first received the fleet operation order when the Flagship "AOBA" of the 16th Squadron came to BANGKA STRAIT from Singapore. What astonished me most about that order was that it specifically stated that "all persons captured should be killed" in order to assure secrecy of our plans. This statement that "all persons captured should be killed" was contained in the main order and details were on the third or fourth page of the "memoranda on verbal explanation by the Chief of Staff", which is contained in the Fleet Operational Order. In every fleet such memoranda was usually distributed to all fleet units as a part of the operation order to show the general lines and details of the execution of the operation. Although the memoranda in question was issued in the name of the Chief of Staff of the fleet, and was mimeographed. I know that in practice such memoranda was usually issued in accordance with the will or order of the C-in-C of the Fleet, who examined and signed them. So in this particular case I looked upon the memorandum as an order from Admiral TAKASU himself. All these documents were bound together and bore a "chop" of the C-in-C.

The fleet Operation Order was a fairly voluminous one and included such operational material as various precautions, weather conditions, enemy's ordinary course, disposition of forces. The order concerning persons captured was written clearly in the third or fourth sheet of the Staff officer's memorandum which was enclosure 1 of the Fleet Order. Also it was clearly stipulated therein that "the Captain and a part of the officers, as well as those connected with communications, anti-submarine weapons and air force, from whom useful information may be obtained will be examined at Fleet H.Qs".

The order of the 16th Squadron was relatively simple and was in mimeographed long hand. The only thing that I remember about it now is that it was very similar in policy to the Fleet Operational Order, and it repeated the paragraph about the disposal of captured persons.

On the afternoon of 9th March, when my ship joined the Flag-ship "AOBA" after sinking the "BEHAR", I made a report by signal of the circumstances of the sinking, the main dimensions of the vessel, her general course and the nationalities and number of captured persons. Whereupon Commander MOMOCHIYO SHIMANOUCHI, Senior Staff Officer of the 16th Squadron, signalled to me. "Request for purpose of future reference, a detailed report regarding the reasons for the sinking of the SS "BEHAR" also persons captured are to be disposed of as soon as possible in accordance with the Fleet Order". I gave my explanation by signal, adding that "persons captured are now being examined".

On the afternoon of the 10th March, when examination of captured persons aboard my ship was almost finished, I made the following proposal by signal to the Commander of the 16th Squadron, "I believe it is proper that the captured persons should not be killed on board, but rather that the English men be employed in construction of air-fields and Indian captured persons as crew of motor barges", but immediately came the signal from the Flagship "AOBA" (Source of origin Admiral SAKONJU) "Captured persons should be killed immediately as stipulated in Fleet Order". The execution took place at about midnight of March 18/19 and after it was completed I received a report from the officer in charge of the execution (Lt. ISHIHARA) of his having full precautions not to have caused the captured persons previous fear or unnecessary suffering, and due measures taken for their burial at sea.

The "TONE" was a cruiser of 8,500 tons displacement and had a complement of 85 officers and 1,100 ratings.

It was usual to carry sufficient victuals on board for a period of two months. This would consist of Rice, Barley, Dried Fish, Dried Vegetable, Pickles, Bean Paste, Oil, Fat. At the time of the sinking of the "BEHAR" I estimate there were on board sufficient reduced rations for a period of five days.

The captured persons received the same rations as my own ship's company, with an addition of stew and biscuits. The water purifying system was such that there would be sufficient water for the prisoners to have a small ration daily. The shortage was caused by lack of fuel.

The statement has been read over to me by an interpreter and is a true and correct transcript of what I have said, to the whole of which statement I now append my signature.

Signed at Stanley Gaol. This 12th day of March, 1947.

Signature.................................
Name in block letters :   MAYAZUMI HARUO

SWORN Before me:

Signature: E.C.Watson   Captain.
WAR CRIMES INVESTIGATION UNIT,
HONG KONG.

The following affidavit was made on 12th March 1947 by the Captain of the "TONE"

FURTHER STATEMENT OF MAYUZUMI, HARUO

1. I was ordered by Vice-Admiral SAKONJU on 16th March, 1944, to carry out the execution of the survivors on board TONE on the 18th of March, 1944 after I had cleared Batavia. I told him that if it had to be done, I would see that it was done as humanely as possible. He agreed.

2. I reported the execution to the staff of 16th Squadron on the morning of 20th March from Singapore and Vice-Admiral SAKONJU must have known about it, although I did not make a signal at the time of the execution.

3. The TONE was still under the command of the 16th Squadron at the time of the execution. I believe that the TONE did not leave the 16th Squadron until 20th March at Singapore. If the operation was declared completed on the 16th March and TONE relieved of its duties with the 16th Squadron then MII's efforts on 17th March in obtaining permission for the release of a number of Indian survivors would not have been directed to the Commander of the 16th Squadron.

4. The signalled order of March 10th from the AOBA read approximately as follows: "Meirei Dori Tadachi ni Shobun Seyo" "Dispose of them immediately in accordance with order". I suppose this order was issued for security purposes, as it was felt that if prisoners were landed they would be in a position to divulge information and as the Fleet Operation Order had given this order.

5. I met Cmdr. ARASE at the Second Demobilisation Ministry. He was gunnery officer of the AOBA at the time of the incident. He remembered the operational order issued by the 16th Squadron but did not remember

clearly that issued by the Southwest Area Fleet.

6. The execution started at about 2200 hours 18th March 1944. It lasted for approximately 3 hours. I gave orders that no one was to be allowed to witness the execution on the quarterdeck. When I went to the quarterdeck for a short while just before the execution had commenced, I spoke to ISHIHARA and transmitted the order of Admiral SAKONJU I could see very little as it was a dark night. I did see ISHIHARA and the forms of KINOSHITA and YOSHIOKA. I was afraid that if others were included they would not carry it out in a proper manner. I believe that the execution was conducted in as humane a manner as possible.

7. The following officers were on board the TONE at the time of the execution:

Cmdr.	MII Junsuke	1st Lieutenant (Executive Officer)
Lt/Cmdr	TANI	Gunnery Officer
Lt/Cmdr	UTSUMI	Damage control and Divisional Officer
Lt/Cmdr	ASANO	Torpedo Officer
Lt	NODA	W/T Officer
Lt	KIMURA	Divisional Officer
Comm.	NAKAYA	Engineer
Sub/Lt	TAKEUCHI	Assistant Engineer
Lt/Cmdr	NAKAHASHI	Chief Medical Officer
Lt	NAGAI	Chief Paymaster
Lt (res)	MORIMOTO	Seamanship Branch
Special Sub/Lt	OGAWA	Boiler Divisional Officer
Sub/Lt	YOSHIOKA	
Lt	ISHIHARA	Master At Arms**
Sub/Lt	KINOSHITA	Assistant Master At Arms**
Sub/Lt	OTSUKA	

(Pay)	Sub/Lt	AKAISHI	Captain's Secretary
	Sub/Lt	SUSUKI	Machine Guns
(Surg)	Sub/Lt	KANO	Ass't Medical Officer
(Pay)	Sub/Lt	OYABU	(Reservist)
	Sub/Lt	AKITA	Ass't Navigating Officer
	Sub/Lt	TANAKA	Watchkeeping Officer
	Sub/Lt	SHINKO	Eng. Divisional Officer
	Sub/Lt	UEHARA	Ass't Engineer

8. Excluding the execution party there should have been no witnesses. Everyone on board knew that the execution had taken place. The blood on the quarterdeck was washed down with fire hoses probably on the following morning.

The statement has been read over to me by an interpreter and is a true and correct transcript of what I have said, to the whole of which statement I now append my signature.

Signed at Stanley Gaol. This _____ day of March, 1947

Signature: Mayuzuni - Haruo
Name in block letters: MAYUZUMI HARUO

SWORN BEFORE ME

Signature: E.C.Watson, Captain
War Crimes Investigation Unit,
HONG KONG.

This 12th day of March 1947.

An Officer detailed to examine the above by the Commander-In-Chief, Allied Land Forces, South East Asia.
Authy: ALFSEA War Crimes Instruction No.1, 2nd Edition, para 19a.

Author's note.
*** This information obtained from Affidavit of ISHIHARA Takonari 14.5.49*

Affidavit sworn by Captain Mayuzumi Haruo 17.3.47

My name is MAYUZUMI HARUO. I was formerly a Captain in the Imperial Japanese Navy and was appointed captain of the cruiser "TONE" on December 1st 1943 and I joined the ship at Kure on December 4th 1943.

Movements of TONE and record of Incidents Leading up to Execution of Survivors of M.V.BEHAR, on 18 March 1944.

27.2.44 Received Operation Order from AOBA, flagship of 16th Squadron, issued by Admiral S.TAKASU Commander-in-Chief, Southwest Area Fleet. I do not remember the date of the Fleet Operational Order, but it was signed by Admiral TAKASU. In Appendix 1 of this Order was a directive as to treatment of survivors of enemy ships sunk. All members of the crew and passengers were to be killed with the exception of Radar, anti-submarine, W/T, and Aerial Operations personnel, who were to be picked up for interrogation. Left LINGA FOR BANGKA.

28.2.44 With Rear-Admiral SAKONJU on board his flagship AOBA, decided details of operation. Ships within 200 miles of COCOS Islands were to be boarded by a prize crew. Ships outside this area were to be sunk.

1.3.44   Passed through SUNDA Straits.

4.3.44   200 miles east of COCOS.

9.3.44   800 miles bearing 190 degrees or 200 degrees from COCOS. 1130 HRS sank M.V. BEHAR by gunfire 2000 yards. Behar ordered to stop and not to send out W/T messages. Behar did not stop and no answer to signal. First salvo fired 300 yards ahead. Behar changed course. Second salvo hit ship. Lifeboats seen leaving ship on port side. Order to cease fire given. When lifeboats well away from ship, fired salvo at about 2000 yards. Ship listed to starboard and sank quickly, probably because crew opened Kingston valves. Survivors picked up by TONE's 2 lifeboats:-

40 English, including 2 women. One lady was the wife of a banker, about 45 years of age, and was proceeding to India via Australia from Singapore. The other lady was the wife of an engineer (civil) aged about 35 years and had come from Shanghai.

About 40 Indians, mostly crew.
2 Chinese seamen.
1 Chinese Agricultural Expert, Dr. CHING.

1400 HOURS JOINED THE AOBA and reported by signal. Received signal from Senior Staff Officer Commander SHIMANOUCHI, 16th Squadron, to treat persons captured in accordance with Fleet Operational Order: "Dispose of them immediately in accordance with Order", answered that prisoners were in process of being interrogated.

10.3.44 P.M. Signalled to Rear-Admiral SAKONJU proposing prisoners should not be killed but Englishmen be used for construction of airfields and Indians used as crews for small motor barges. SAKONJU replied "Must act in accordance with Fleet Operational Order immediately". Decided to propose again in Batavia so did not reply to signal. By that time interrogation conducted by Lt.(Pay) NAGAI was finished. Lt. ISHIWARA was placed in charge of prisoners. Sug. Lt. Commander NAKAHASHI examined captured persons every day. Prisoners were quartered in 2 large cabins on lower deck port quarter, below officer's sick bay. The English women had a partitioned enclosure in the forward cabin, with separate heads. These women received every consideration and their property and hand-bags were placed in a place of safety on my instructions and the M.O. was instructed to treat them in a manner suitable to European LADIES.

13.3.44 When about 200 miles off COCOS it was feared that aircraft from aircraft carriers based at Trinco or Colombo and cruisers would cut off their retreat. The AOBA was small and did not carry much fuel and the maximum speed was about 15 knots. When the Behar was sunk she sent out RRRR by W/T. Some of the Tone's officers thought that they should comply with orders and kill the prisoners, but on the other hand most of my officers thought my idea was right. Commander MII agreed with me. The Tone was newly equipped by 35-25 mm machine guns with not sufficient increase in crew. I felt my responsibility keenly as in the event of action every man was required at his action station and no man could really be spared to guard the prisoners. As the prisoners were made up mostly of seafaring men, they could obviously do great damage in an action if left unguarded. There were a large number of damage control valves installed in the lower decks. If we were sunk in action and the prisoners escaped and were rescued they would be in a position to give away valuable information, and on this point the secret operational order was quite emphatic. While rounding the Cocos Islands, Commander Mii reported to me that numerous unidentified signals and electrical impulses were intercepted from Ceylon and Australia, which probably meant that enemy forces were approaching and all the officers on board were becoming uneasy. Fresh water was getting short and all fresh food had been consumed. I told him that the officers and crew would have to bear the hardships as I was determined to make Batavia with the prisoners on board.

15.3.44 Arrived at TANDJONG PRIOK at 1900 Tokyo time, about 1 hour before sunset. I immediately went on board the flagship and reported that the prisoners had not been killed and that in my opinion the prisoners should not be killed but made to work as suggested previously. For this suggestion I was rebuked by two Staff Officers (SHIMANOUCHI and OYAMADA). The commander of the squadron understood my feelings but because of the Fleet Order, could not change his decision. I experienced a sense of failure but determined to try once again on the next day at a gathering of officers. I was ordered to send the Master of the Behar and 2 or 3 others to the flagship for further interrogation. I understood that the 2 women were not to be included in this number so tried to persuade Rear-Admiral SAKONJU to save them, as it was pitiful to treat them as prisoners. He asked me if there was anything suspicious about them, as women do not travel in wartime unless they were on a military mission. He permitted me to include the women when I told him that there was absolutely nothing suspicious about them. I ordered the Chief Paymaster who had conducted the interrogation to include as many prisoners as possible in the number to be sent to the flagship, and I personally indicated the persons concerned. As far as I can remember the following 16 persons were on the list:– 2 women, Master, Chief Engineer, Chief Officer, 2nd Officer, Radio Officer, Dr. Ching, a naval AB probably an anti-submarine rating, 1 army gunner, 1 petty officer D.C. 1 petty officer anti-submarine, 2 NCO RNZAF, 1 petty officer radar and the Master of a ship which had rescued Japanese air pilots in the China Sea in September 1937.

16.3.44 Sent the prisoners to the Aoba but felt anxious as the number was about 3 times that asked by the Staff Officer. I knew that the lady prisoners were given back their passports, cheque books, and other papers. I found that the others who were taken to the flagship were wearing rings, etc., and was satisfied that nothing had been taken away from them. A full list of the captured persons on forms prescribed by the Fleet was sent to the flagship. At the conference, I again brought up the subject of the captured persons, but was given the same answer. Afterwards I was asked by SHIMANOUCHI and

OYAMADA to explain my course from Batavia to Singapore and they studied soundings and distance from shore and directed that when I was more than 40 miles from land with a sounding of more 20 fathoms in open sea I was to carry out the execution. SHIMANOUCHI repeated these instruction to Rear-Admiral SAKONJU and when I again protested to Sakonju he said; "I understand your position but the orders are from the C-in-C in his Operational Order for operational purposes and you must act as you have been instructed". I felt this was a very definite order. On the 16th evening, I was invited to a dinner given by Lt. Gen. HARADA, the Army Officer commanding Batavia and on the 17th I went to a dinner given by the Senior Naval Officer, Capt. MAEDA, and at these functions could not discuss the captured persons question with Sakonju and I knew that I had failed.

17.3.44 While at lunch at a Japanese restaurant in Batavia with GOTO Gonzo, a retired Naval Captain, at the time connected with the Batavia Branch of the Kawasaki Dockyard, my executive officer Commander Mii, reported to me that Admiral Sakonju had refused to entertain a proposal to obtain permission to land prisoners. Commander MII met Rear-Admiral Sakonju at the residence of Mr. YOSHIOKA, the Senior Civil Officer at the Naval Headquarters. The proposal was put up to the Rear-Admiral who then gave permission to land a few Indians, but no others. I commended MII for his efforts and ordered him to send as many as possible ashore as I had previous engagements to look over Captain Goto's dockyards and to attend Capt.Maeda's dinner and could not get back to the Tone. After this dinner Comdr. Mii informed me that SHIMANOUCHI would not change the order and I had another interview with Rear-Admiral SAKONJU, and repeated my request for the order to be changed but he refused.

18.3.44 I arrived on board "TONE" at 1400 hours and I was handed a signal authorising the landing of about ten

Indians and was informed that twenty had been landed whilst I was ashore. Mii surmised that the Commander of the Squadron had thought that no leakage of information would result from the transfer of a few uneducated Indian seaman ashore. Left Batavia for Singapore in company with CHIKUMA, with Capt. NORIMITSU as the senior officer of the Division. The Java Sea was unsafe due to submarines and aircraft operating from the Indian Ocean. Entrances to Tandjong Priok and Bangka Straits were dangerous submarine zones. The execution could not be carried out in the Bangka Straits as we could be seen from the shores. It was decided that the best place was about 40 or 50 miles from Batavia. I delayed the order for the execution as I had hopes that there would be a change in the situation or that I may be ordered to transfer the prisoners to a cargo ship or transport. I regret that no such change materialised. At 2200 hours Tokyo time, 3 hours before reaching Bangka Straits, I transmitted the Admiral's order to Lt. Ishihara. At about 1700 hours Tokyo time before we left Batavia I told Lt. Ishihara that I had orders to carry out the execution. The method of execution was to see that it was carried out with least possible pain and suffering and it was suggested that the execution should take place at night. The prisoners being taken out one by one as if for further interrogation, then knocked unconscious and killed while still in that state. The execution must be carried out by a well educated graduate of the Naval College so as to avoid cruelty and so that there would be no failure due to lack of knowledge of weapons used. Courteous treatment of the bodies was ordered. A sword was to be thrust through the heart to assure death. The use of fire-arms forbidden because of flash and sound. All this was explained to me by OYAMADA on 16.3.44. Just before reaching Bangka Straits I received a report from Ishihara that the execution had been carried out in accordance with OYAMADA's suggestion. I heard a sword had been used to cut the jugular vein and a thrust was made into the heart to ensure against failure. There were several members in the execution party but I can only remember the names of two officers; Sub Lt. KINOSHITA and Acting Sub Lt. YOSHIOKA. I did not witness the execution as I was on the bridge all the time. I erased the record of the signals in the signals record book referring to the prisoners and the execution from the reports sent to the 16th Squadron, 7th Squadron and the Southwest Fleet, in case the book should fall into enemy hands. I sent a written report of the execution to SAKONJU's and TAKASU's H.Q.s

In May 1944, Shimanouchi and Oyamada informed me in Singapore that they had received these written reports.

The last time I met ISHIHARA TAKANORI was in early March or the end of February 1946. I met him at the Second Demobilisation Ministry, Tokyo, when he was called in for interrogation with regard to the "Behar" case. He was living in a room within the Ministry whilst he was being interrogated.

We discussed the "Behar" incident, Ishihara said that as he was ordered to execute the prisoners on "SAKONJU's orders he thought that he should not be involved in the matter as he had no responsibility at all. He was very upset about the investigation. We did not discuss what we would say when we were to be interrogated by the Allied Powers. He did not tell me what he would do in case he was involved in the matter. The only persons known to me who were members of the execution party are the following: Ishihara, who was in charge of the party, Yoshioka and Kinoshita, who are both dead and possibly Akeuchi who was not busy in the Engine Room at the time of the execution.

I think that I stated previously that I had passed the order for the execution of the prisoners through Mii. I now think that I gave detailed instructions to Ishihara in my cabin.

Mii has no responsibility whatsoever in this case.

The above statement has been read over to me by an interpreter and is a true and correct transcript of what I have said, to the whole of which statement I now append

86

my signature.

Signed at Stanley Gaol this 17th day of March 1947.

Mayuzumi Haruo.

SWORN BEFORE ME: E.C. Watson Capt.

On completion of the Military Court trial, on 29th October 1947 the court found Rear Admiral Sakonju guilty and sentenced him to death, and Captain Mayazumi was also found guilty, but took into consideration that he had made several attempts to save the prisoners lives, he was sentenced to 7 years imprisonment.

The findings being subject to confirmation. The prisoners defence council making a petition against the sentences.

From examination of the affidavits submitted by Captain Mayazumi and Rear-Admiral Sakonju it can be seen that very conflicting evidence emerges as to the version of events leading up to the executions, but certainly it does appear from Japanese witnesses, that the Captain of the "TONE" did make serious efforts to have the disposal order for the prisoners annulled. What is not explained is why "Operation Sayo No.1" was so special and top secret from any other Japanese naval action, that all survivors had to be executed. Mayazumi's version of how the prisoners were treated on board his ship does not in the least tally with the accounts supplied by the prisoners, which clearly will have been registered at the Military Trial.

The Judge Advocate General of the Far East Land Forces duly considered the Petition and sent the following letter to the Commander Land Forces HONG KONG:

BM/JAG/65287
OFFICE OF THE DJAG
General Headquarters,
Far East Land Forces.

17th December 1947.

<u>Commander Land Forces HONG KONG</u>

Subject   War Crimes Trial

1.   Reference the proceedings of the trial of

1. Rear Admiral SAKONJU Naomasa

2. Capt. MAYAZUMI Haruo

Both of the Imperial Japanese Navy and the attached petitions.
2. The accused were tried by Military Court at Hong Kong on 19th September 1947 on a charge for committing a war crime in that they were concerned in the killing of approximately 65 survivors from the sinking of the armed merchantman "BEHAR". Both accused pleaded not guilty but were convicted and sentenced to death and 7 years respectively.

3. The fact of the case are briefly as follows:

The accused Admiral was at the relevant time in command of the 16th Squadron for Operation Sayo No. 1. The object of the operation was to disrupt Allied communications in the Indian Ocean and the Squadron received its orders at a conference on the flagship in the Bangka Straits.

4. The main outlines of the orders were that where possible Allied ships were to be captured and taken to a

friendly port. Where this was not feasible i.e. if (inter alia) captured more than 200 miles from the Cocos Islands, the ship was to be sunk. The minimum number of prisoners were to be taken for intelligence purposes.

5. Accordingly the operation progressed and the "Tone" sighted and sank the "Behar" on 9th March 1944 approximately 600 miles from the Cocos Islands, rescuing almost everybody aboard. A signal was made to the flagship reporting the incident and an order was received to dispose of all save the minimum number of prisoners according to plan. As a result of the commander of the "Tone" failing to comply with that order a further signal was received from the flagship the next day (10th March) ordering immediate disposal. This too was ignored and the Squadron eventually arrived at its base, Batavia, on the 15th March. On the 16th March a study conference was held on the "Aoba" and on the 18th the "Tone" left for Singapore with some survivors of the "Behar" on board who were killed en route.

6. During the course of the trial evidence was given that at the Conference in the Bangka Strait, the Captain queried the orders regarding the "disposal" of prisoners. Even by the end of the trial it is not made unequivocally clear as to whether that order came in the Fleet Orders and was repeated in Squadron Orders or whether it originated in the Squadron Orders. It is not however denied that two signals were made and received ordering the immediate disposal of prisoners on the 9th and 10th or that prisoners were in fact disposed of on board the "Tone" on the 18th en route for Singapore.

7. The Captain's defence was that he protested against those orders from the start and continued to maintain his views in spite of the signals in order that he might approach the Admiral and ask that they be changed. He said that he did so in Batavia and that his 2nd in Command did so too but whereas he was unsuccessful in his quest the latter managed to arrange for the landing

approximately 20 survivors at Batavia. The Admiral ordered the disposal of the rest to be effected by him en route to Singapore and he had in the end no alternative but to comply.

8. The Admiral said that instructions as to disposal of prisoners was in accordance with Fleet Orders and he did not deny making the signals of the 9th and 10th. However he maintains that no serious efforts were made to see him by the Captain at Batavia and that he only saw him to speak to at the study conference. He insisted that though displeased with the Captain's conduct, on arrival at Batavia, the dire emergency which existed at sea owing to possible enemy attack and the menaces of prisoners on board a fighting ship had ceased and he therefore ordered all prisoners to be landed there and presumed that was done. His next point was that after the study conference the operation was over and signals were received detaching the "Tone" and reverting her to her Home Squadron. Thus when she sailed on the 18th there was no chain of command between himself and her captain and the killing of the prisoners. then was entirely the responsibility of the Captain.

9. The Captain called evidence to show that he was not yet aware of the transfer which he thought improbable on the 18th. In any case the killing was done on the completion of the chain of command given while he was with the 16th Squadron.

10. There is much conflicting evidence as to the exact position of the "Tone" after the 16th and as to whether the Admiral was personally seen by the Captain and stuck to his original orders or whether he modified them making the actual killing the responsibility of the Captain.

11. The court must have believed that the Admiral insisted on his orders being complied with and that the Captain was to blame to the extent of carrying out those orders which they both admitted to knowing to be

contrary to International Law. The evidence was sufficient to support the findings.

12. Certificate B fails to make clear whether or not the death sentence was passed unanimously in accordance with paragraph 9 of the Regulations for the trial of War Criminals. If the President is able to confirm that paragraph 9 was complied with the Proceedings may be confirmed; otherwise the sentence is illegal and the Court will have to be reassembled to pass sentence afresh on Rear Admiral Sakonju.

13. The petitions disclose no material factors not before the court but stress the bona fides of the accused, their personal dislike of the orders regarding disposal of prisoners and their personal private affairs.

   I advise that the Petitions be dismissed

                         Brigadier,
           DJAG, Far East Land Forces.

Author's Note.
The Signature of the Brigadier is unreadable.
Rear Admiral Sakonju Naomasa was duly hanged at Stanley Gaol Hong Kong on 21st January 1948.

Sources of information

PRO KEW WO 311/564 WO 235/1089 WO 311/549

The following letter was sent to the Ministry of Transport from the Judge Advocate General's Office.

From : Lieutenant-Colonel G. Barratt.

MD/JAG/FS/JM/23(2G)

Office of :

The Judge Advocate General,
6, Spring Gardens,
Cockspur Street,
LONDON S.W.1.

7 February 1948

Dear

Thank you for your letter No. M. 14553/45 dated 3 February 1948.

I can now give you a certain amount of information with regard to the trial which has recently been received in this office and which may be of some use to you.

The accused were, as you are doubtless aware, Admiral SAKONJU (who was incidentally, hanged on Wednesday, 21 January 1948) and Captain MIYAZUMI. These accused were tried by Military Court at Hong Kong on 19 September 1947 on a charge of committing a war crime in that they were concerned in the killing of approximately 65 survivors from the sinking of the armed Merchantman "Behar". Both accused pleaded not guilty but were convicted and sentenced to death and to seven years' imprisonment respectively.

The accused Admiral was at the relevant time in command of the 16 Squadron flying his flag in the "Aoba". The "Tone" of the 7th Squadron with the accused Captain in command was at that time attached to the 16th Squadron on a special operation which was designed to disrupt Allied communications in the Indian Ocean.

The orders for this operation were that where possible Allied ships were to be captured and taken to a friendly port. Where this was not possible, as for instance, if they were captured more than 200 miles from the Cocos Islands, the ship or ships were to be sunk. The minimum number of prisoners was to be taken for intelligence purposes.

During the course of this operation the "Tone" sighted and sank the "Behar" on 9 March 1944 approximately 600 miles from the Cocos Islands. Almost all of the passengers and crew were rescued. A signal was made to the flagship reporting the incident and an order was received in the "Tone" to dispose of all save the minimum number of prisoners according to plan. As a result of the commander of the "Tone" failing to comply with that order a further signal was received from the flagship next day (10 March 1944) ordering immediate compliance. This too was ignored and the Squadron eventually arrived at its base at Batavia on 15 March. On 16 March a conference was held on the "Aoba" and on 18 March the "Tone" left for Singapore with some of the survivors of the "Behar" on board who were killed en route.

During the trial evidence was given that Captain MIYAZUMI queried the orders regarding the disposal of the prisoners. Even by the end of the trial it was not made unequivocally clear as to whether these orders came in the Fleet Orders and were repeated in Squadron Orders or whether they were in fact originated in the Squadron Orders. It was not, however, denied that two signals were made and received ordering the immediate disposal of the prisoners on 9 and 10 March or that the prisoners were in fact disposed of on board the "Tone" on 18 March en route for Singapore.

The Captain's defence was that he protested against these orders from the start and continued to protest in order that he might have a chance to approach the Admiral personally and ask that they be changed. He stated that he did so in Batavia and that his second in command did so too. But whereas he was unsuccessful in his quest the latter managed to arrange for the landing of approximately 20 survivors at Batavia. The Admiral ordered the disposal of the rest to be carried out by him en route for Singapore and he had no alternative but to comply. The Admiral in his defence stated that the orders as to the disposal of the prisoners was in accordance with Fleet Orders and he did not deny making the signals on 9 and 10 March. He maintained that no serious effort was made by the Captain to approach him at Batavia on this matter. He insisted that though displeased with the Captain's conduct, by the time they had arrived at Batavia the possibility of meeting Allied fighting ships had ceased and he therefore ordered all prisoners to be landed there and he presumed that had been done. His next point was that after the conference at Batavia on 16 March the "Tone" had been detached from his command and had reverted to her home Squadron and that therefore the killing of the prisoners on board the "Tone" on 18 March was entirely the Captain's responsibility. The Captain called evidence to show that he had no information as to this transfer of command and that anyway the killing was done as the result of an order which he received when he was under command of the 16th Squadron.

Despite a considerable amount of conflicting evidence as to the exact position of the "Tone" after the 16 March the Court must have believed that the Admiral insisted upon his orders being complied with and that the Captain was to blame to the extent of carrying out these orders which they both admitted knowing to be contrary to International Law. The evidence was sufficient to support the findings.

It is unfortunate that the missing Europeans were not accounted for individually but it was established that those who were put ashore at Batavia included "key" men such as the master and others who could supply information of interest to the Japanese.

Perhaps you will let me know if there is any other information on this subject which you require

Yours,
G.BARRATT

G.A. Inge Esq.,
Ministry of Transport,
Berkeley Square House,
London W.1

Source PRO KEW WO 311/564

MAY 1949

With the hanging of Rear-Admiral Sakonju, that would have appeared to be the end of "BEHAR" affair, but on 14th May 1949 Lieutenant ISHIHARA Takanori, the former Master At Arms of the "TONE" was in the hands of War Crimes Investigation team in Japan, and made a sworn statement before W. Slater an honorary Major, employed as an interpreter at British Minor War Crimes S.C.A.P. (Supreme Command Allied Powers) Tokyo.

SWORN STATEMENT OF ISHIHARA TAKANORI MASTER AT ARMS ON CRUISER "TONE"

I, ISHIHARA Takonari, having been duly sworn on oath make the following statement:–

I have been duly warned that I am not obliged to make any statement but that anything I say will be taken down in writing and may be used in evidence. I voluntarily make the following statement:–

1. Name:	ISHIHARA Takonari
2. Nationality:	Japanese.
3. Age:	31 Yrs. Date of Birth 9 March 1919
4. Present Address:	Kagoshima-shi, Yamashita-cho, No. 84
5. Registered Domicile:	Kagoshima-ken, Oshima-gun, Ryuyo-mura, Ishihara No. 6.
6. Present occupation:	Unemployed.
7. Date of Demobilisation:	August 1945.
8. Rank	Former Naval Lieutenant.

9. War Service Record:

Dec.1941 to Apr. 1942	Navigating Officer, Destroyer SHIRAGUMO.
Apr. 1942 to Aug. 1942	Navigating Officer, Destroyer ARARE
Aug.1942 to Nov. 1942	Navigating Officer, Destroyer NATSUGUMO
Nov.1942 to Oct. 1943	Divisional Officer, 9th Division Warship YAMATO
Oct. 1943 to Feb. 1945	Divisional Officer, 2nd Division, Warship TONE
Feb. 1945 to Aug. 1945	Instructor Naval Academy.

10. While I was in the Warship TONE during 1944 (day and month not remembered) we sank a British Merchantman "BEHAR" off the West Coast of Australia. About 60 of the crew were interned in the "TONE". After making BATAVIA about 40 of the crew of the "BEHAR" were landed at BATAVIA. While the TONE was proceeding to Singapore, in the vicinity of BANGKA Sea, the remaining crew members of the "BEHAR" were disposed of in accordance with a strict order from the Captain of the TONE. The bodies were buried at sea. The method of disposal was ordered by the ship's Captain, CAPTAIN MAYUZUMI to the ship's First Lieutenant, COMMANDER MII. At that time I was the Master at Arms, and this order was passed on to me by the First Lieutenant. I ordered the Assistant Master at Arms, Sub-Lieutenant KINOSHITA, to carry out the execution. During the night they were brought up one by one to the quarterdeck where members of the Judo class (number not remembered) rendered them unconscious by blows, when members of the Japanese fencing class (number not remembered) cut them with swords. I, as the Master at Arms at that time, was not in agreement with the strict order of the Captain of the ship with regard to the disposal of the crew of the "BEHAR", and stated my disagreement. At that time I was also in charge of the

96

anti-aircraft machine guns, and as it was necessary to keep a good look out for submarines I was on the quarterdeck for only a short while at the beginning of the execution, and later took up my position at the anti-aircraft stations to keep a look out for submarines. Towards the end of the execution I again went to the quarterdeck. I recollect that while the execution was being carried out the Assistant Master at Arms was on the quarterdeck in charge of the execution, from beginning to end. Towards the end of the execution I went to the quarterdeck where I also cut one member of the crew of the "BEHAR" with a sword.

I, ISHIHARA Takonori, swear upon oath that I have written the fore-going statement truthfully and conscientiously, adding nothing and concealing nothing whatsoever. I now voluntarily append my signature to this statement..

TOKYO 14th May, 1949.   (Signed)   ISHIHARA Takonori.

                             (Imprint of right thumb)

Subscribed and sworn to before me by ISHIHARA Takonari, this 14th day of May 1949 at Tokyo.
                    Signed. W.Salter
                    Hon. Major.
                    British Division,
                    Legal Section,
                    G.H.Q., S.C.A.P.
Translated by W. Salter. Hon. Major. 16.5.49
The following letter accompanied the affidavit to the War Office in London

Source PRO KEW WO 311/549

                             Office of the Deputy
                    Director of Army Legal Services.
                         General Headquarters,
                         Far East Land Forces,

15th July 1949.

BM/WCS.50738
CONFIDENTIAL.

Director of Army Legal Services,
The War Office,
Hotel Victoria,
Northumberland Avenue,
LONDON W.C.2.

BEHAR TONE CASE

ISHIHARA TAKONORI.

Reference my Signal 22009 WCS of 20th May 1949.

1. I forward herewith the evidence in this case. It consists of two proofs by Captain MAYAZUMI HARUO together with evidence on Affidavit by one WILLIAM SALTER now in England.

2. The facts of the case are very short. In March 1944 a Japanese Cruiser known as "The Tone" sank a British Merchantman "The Behar" off the west coast of Australia. At the time Captain MAYAZUMI HARUO was in command of "The Tone".

3. Some 65 Survivors from the "The Behar" were taken aboard "The Tone" and executed on the Quarterdeck of this vessel on the night 18/19 March 1944.

4. Captain MAYAZUMI HARUO was ordered by his Vice Admiral one SAKONJI to carry out the executions.

The orders having been relayed to ISHIHARA TAKANORI, Master at Arms, he in his turn appears to have relayed them still further to his Assistant Master at Arms who perpetrated the bulk of the executions.

ISHIHARA TAKANORI however in a confession to WILLIAM SALTER above mentioned admits to carrying out one execution himself.

5. If this case were to go to trial the Prosecution evidence would consist of Captain MAYAZUMI HARUO together with an Affidavit of WILLIAM SALTER exhibiting a confession by the accused.

6. On the assumption you found yourself in a position to advise trial I have ascertained the wishes of the Commander-in-Chief. They are against a trial on the grounds that the events concerned, if they occurred at all, indeed occurred more than five years ago coupled with the fact that at the material time the accused was but an underling in the matter.

7. I would conclude by saying that Captain MAYAZUMI HARUO is now undergoing a sentence of 7 years imprisonment as a result of a sentence passed upon him in October 1947 by War Crimes Court for his part in this matter whilst Vice-Admiral SAKONJI is, on my present information, deceased having been hanged as a result of the sentence passed upon him by the Court which dealt with Captain MAYAZUMI HARUO.

8. I shall be glad of your instructions.

(Signed) G.A.WHITELEY
Lt-Col,
Deputy Director of Army Legal Services
Far East Land Forces.
G.A.WHITELEY

Source PRO KEW WO 311/549.

It is surprising, that the top level of legal services in Singapore have incorrectly spelt the name of the Japanese Rear-Admiral who was hanged for his part in ordering the executions. Even more surprising is the wording of the wishes of the Commander-in-Chief referred to in paragraph 6:

"They are against a trial on the grounds that the events concerned, if they occurred at all, indeed occurred more than five years ago........". How could there have ever been any doubt about whether or not the events occurred? The British military trial held in Hong Kong conclusively proved they did, Rear-Admiral Sakonju being hanged in January 1948 as a result of being found guilty.

Paragraph 7 appears to be rather strangely worded "Rear-Admiral SAKONJI is, on my present information, deceased having been hanged as a result of the sentence passed upon him........".

By 1949 the will to prosecute the Japanese for war crimes was dimishing, in no small part due to pressure from the Americans, who in turn were pressured by the Japanese who wanted such cases against the Japanese Military dropped, as the price for ensuring that Japan became a western style democracy with a leadership of pro- American leaning, thus helping to contain the spread of communism that was spreading in the Far East. This change of policy by the Americans must have been at the highest level of political and military circles, and the British Government followed the American line.

A reply to the letter of 15th July 1949 from the Far East Land Forces was swiftly replied to by the legal department of the Army, which ensured that no war crimes charges would be progressed against Ishihara Takanori, the Master At Arms on the cruiser "TONE" who was in charge of the execution of the 69 prisoners held on board the vessel. The following is a copy of that reply.

Directorate of Army Legal Services
Telegrams: Troopers

Abbey 1272 Ext 350

DALS/FS/JC/163

2 August 1949

A.D.A.L.S.
G.H.Q.
FARELF.

Ishihara Takanori.

(Behar Tone Case).

Reference your minute BM/WCS/50738 dated 15 July 1949 submitting the papers in this case.

1. I am unable to advise that there is no evidence to justify the trial of the above-named, I note from para 6 of your minute that the Commander-in-Chief is not desirous of re-starting trials after years, particularly where the accused was but an underling at the time. I note that the other persons involved are already serving sentences and it would I think, not be desirable to drag them out of prison and try them for any other offences after this period of time.

2. In the circumstances I too do not think it desirable to bring this person to trial and so I am not advising any charge.

3. I am keeping the papers you forwarded to me in case any question should arise in the future. If you particularly want the papers returned to you perhaps you will let me know.

(Signed) Initials.
Director of Army Legal Services.

(H.SHAPCOTT).

Source PRO KEW WO 311/549

Author's note.
Paragraph 1 of this letter notes that "other persons involved are already serving sentences and it would I think, not be desirable to drag them out of prison and try them for any other offences......". The letter being replied to quite clearly states there is only one person serving a prison sentence".

EPILOGUE

The war crimes investigations in Japan were to affect a "BEHAR" survivor, Lieutenant James Gowing Godwin of the Royal New Zealand Navy in a most unusual set of circumstances.

On repatriation to New Zealand, and following a period of convalescence, Godwin was seconded to the Australian Army because of his knowledge of the Japanese language. He was commissioned with the rank of Lieutenant in the Second New Zealand Expeditionary Force (Japan), commonly known as J-Force in March 1946. The objective of sending him to Japan to work with Supreme Command Allied Powers (S.C.A.P.) to investigate War Crimes on behalf of the Australians, as well as his own country. Godwin rose to the rank of Captain and was attached to the 2 Australian War Crimes Section in Tokyo and later 1 Australian War Crimes Section at Manus. He most diligently investigated Japanese war crimes from 1946 until 1950. However as time went by his investigations, and those of other investigators became hampered by instructions coming from General MacArthur's H.Q. to drop investigations into certain war crimes, and to destroy all papers connected with the same. Thus the war crimes investigation teams were having their efforts to bring justice to Japanese war criminals undermined. This state of affairs becoming more frequent as time progressed, so much so, that Godwin became very disillusioned, and in fact he defied the edict. Secretly he kept copies of the files he was involved with, and when he left Japan in July 1950 shipped them out to New Zealand where they remained safely stored in a tea chest. Following his death in 1995 these papers have now surfaced, and are now in the process of being published.

Godwin was particularly singled out for harsh treatment by the Japanese on board the "TONE", the "SANUKI MARU" and in Japan. The probable reason for this was because of his physical build. He was a tall well built man, who would tower above the average size

Japanese and would be the target for ill treatment. This was an established custom of the Japanese towards such men who became their prisoners.

The "BEHAR" files were kept secret for 30 years, at the Public Records Office, why this should have been the case is hard to justify from the papers discovered. Is part of the reason, to spare the relatives the pain of knowing exactly how their loved ones died, or was it a hidden objective of the government to dampen public anti-Japanese feelings for political reasons? If it was the former reason, then surely relatives already suspected the worst, when they saw from newsreels at the cinemas the pitiful physical condition of released Far East POWs. The stories that POWs had to tell were already circulating in the press concerning their cruel and evil treatment and about countless atrocities they had witnessed. Therefore for most relatives, it is most likely they probably knew deep inside that their loved ones had died in appalling circumstances, but tried to shut out their darkest thoughts.

Perhaps the most likely reason for keeping the files secret was a political decision concerning the long term future stability of Japan in view of events in China and Korea which were unfolding when the war ended. Most certainly ex-prisoners of the Japanese were treated very shabbily by the allied governments, who by signing the Peace Treaty with Japan in 1951, signed away all prisoners chances for obtaining compensation from the Japanese government, or the Japanese making reparation payments to the countries they had attacked with such barbaric savagery.

Files exist in Australian Government archives concerning the "BEHAR" which still have not been released.

APPENDIX 1

BEHAR   MOTORSHIP   O.N. 168497
Port of Registry: LONDON 7,840 gross tons.
Owners: Hain Steamship Co Ltd. London.
Builders: Barclay, Curle & Co Ltd., Glasgow.
Engines: Two – 4 cylinder 2 S.C.S.A. Doxford oil engines by the Shipbuilder.
Speed: 15½ knots
Launched: 24.5.43
Completed August: 1943

British ship "BEHAR" sailed Melbourne 29th February 1944 for Bombay.
Sunk by Japanese cruiser "TONE" 9TH March 1944 in Indian Ocean
position 20.32S 87.10E.
According to Japanese cruiser log book position given as 20.34S 87.00E.

CREW DETAILS FROM SHIP'S ARTICLES.

	Name	Number	Age	Last Abode
CAPTAIN	MAURICE SYMONS	MSC006664	51	GLASGOW
CHIEF OFFICER	WILLIAM PHILLIPS	1107140	38	CARDIFF
2ND OFFICER	GORDON ROWLANDSON	R235131	30	LONDON E10
3RD OFFICER	JAMES ANDERSON	R194539	23	LONDON SE5
4TH OFFICER	JOHN ROBERTSON	R102086	34	BONESS
APPRENTICE	DENYS MATTHEWS	R291756	17	CARDIFF
APPRENTICE	ALAN MOORE	R275767	18	READING
1ST RADIO OFFICER	ARTHUR WALKER	R204726	26	SOUTHALL
2ND RADIO OFFICER	JAMES SMYTH	R269321	19	BELFAST
3RD RADIO OFFICER	HENRY GORDON CUMMING	R205702	23	GLASGOW
CHIEF ENGINEER	JAMES WEIR	487282	58	GLASGOW
2ND ENGINEER	EDWARD McGINNES	R147088	27	GLASGOW
3RD ENGINEER	EAN NIGEL MacCAILEN CAMPBELL	R11362	43	GLASGOW
4TH ENGINEER	JOSEPH CRAIG	1048098	45	ABERDEEN
5TH ENGINEER	PETER LOVE	R185835	26	AIRDRIE
6TH ENGINEER	JOHN BROWN	R291616	21	GLASGOW
7TH ENGINEER	THOMAS MARTIN	R291706	23	GLASGOW
8TH ENGINEER	ROBERT SMITH	R291615	23	GLASGOW

All DEMS crew Royal Navy & Royal Artillery Maritime Regiment personnel
signed on vessel as "Deckhands". No service details shown in ship's
articles.
Service details found from various memorial registers, and Commonwealth
War Graves Commission.
Gun crew.

Name	Rank & Service Number	Age	Branch & Last Abode
WALTER L. GRIFFITHS	PO P/JX 185951	29	DEMS BIRMINGHAM
THOMAS ROBINSON	AB C/JX 248976	23	DEMS TREHARRIS
LEONARD A. CUTHBERT	L/Seaman C/JX 249947	27	DEMS LONDON SE8
THOMAS G. SAUL	AB C/JX 235844	23	DEMS LEAMINGTON SPA
DONALD G.BRINE	AB P/JX 312434	22	DEMS TROWBRIDGE
JACK STEEL HOPE	AB D.JX 550918	20	DEMS RUGBY
KENNETH COOKE	AB D/JX 444481	19	DEMS OPENSHAW
STANLEY PYECROFT	Gnr 11416381	21	4th Maritime Regt NOTTINGHAM
ARTHUR BOWERS	Bdr 6290844	23	4th Maritime Regt LONDON
ALFRED STREET	Gnr 11259712	34	4th Maritime Regt TYCOCH GLAM
NEIL BRODIE	Bdr 3326794	33	1st Maritime Regt CAMPBELTOWN
ALEXANDER RODNEY	Gnr 1656736	37	1st Maritme Regt GREENOCK
CHARLIE RATCLIFFE	SGT 3441983	37	1st Maritime Regt OLDHAM

R.N. Asdic Operators

Name	Rank & Service Number	Age	Branch & Last Abode
CHARLES P.H. KERSHAW	AB D/JX 187547	29	DEMS ILKESTON
ANGUS McCLEOD	AB C/JX 240098	28	DEMS STORNOWAY
ROBERT I. WILLIAMS	AB D/SSX 35901	22	DEMS DYFFRYN
STANLEY ENOCH	AB D/JX 393587	20	DEMS CAERAU GLAM.

INDIAN CREW 61
CHINESE CREW 2

PASSENGER LIST.
Embarked Wellington New Zealand
FLT.SGT. A.D.BARR   RNZAF
LT.S.C.PARKER   RNZNVR
SUB.LT J.G. GODWIN   RNZNVR
SUB.LT. J.R.BENGE   RNNZVR
DR. LAI YUNG LI   Doctor of Agriculture, well known in New Zealand, also a broadcaster.

Embarked Melbourne Australia.
DUNCAN MacGREGOR   Retired British Bank Manager from Kenya. residing in Burwood, Victoria, Australia.
CAPTAIN P.J.GREEN   Master with China Navigation Co. Ltd.
MRS A.C.SHAW   Wife of Calcutta Dockyard Official.
MRS G.PASCHEOVE   Aged about 55 formerly of Singapore.

APPENDIX 2

The following Officers, crew and passenger of the British Motorship BEHAR died on the night of 18/19th March 1944 whilst prisoners of war in Japanese hands on board the cruiser "TONE" after sailing Tandjong Priok for Singapore via the Bangka Straits 18th March 1944.

The names of all these Officers appear on the Merchant Navy Memorial at Tower Hill Gardens, London.

		Age	Dis. No.
ANDERSON J.S.	3RD OFFICER	30	R194539
BROWN J.	6TH ENGINEER	21	R291616
CAMPBELL E.N. MacG	3RD ENGINEER	43	R11362
CRAIG J.R.	4TH ENGINEER	45	1048098
CUMMING. H.G.	3RD RADIO OFFICER	23	R205702
LOVE P.B.	5TH ENGINEER	26	R185835
McGINNES E.	2ND ENGINEER	27	R147088
MARTIN T.	7TH ENGINEER	23	R291706
MATTHEWS D.J	APPRENTICE	17	R291756
MOORE A.C.	APPRENTICE	18	R275767
ROBERTSON J.	4TH OFFICER	34	R102086
ROWLANDSON G.R.	2ND OFFICER	30	R235131
SMITH R.	8TH ENGINEER	23	R291615
SMYTH J.H.	2ND RADIO OFFICER	19	R269321

DEMS Personnel
LEONARD ALEXANDER CUTHBERT   Chatham Memorial
Leading Seaman C/JX 249947 age 27   Panel 74 Col 3
son of Frederick & Marion Cuthbert. Husband of   President III
Lily Gertrude Cuthbert Deptford London
DIED 19TH March 1944

THOMAS GEORGE SAUL   Chatham Memorial
AB C/JX 235844 age 23   Panel 76 Col 1
son of Thomas & Beatrice M. Saul. Husband of   President III
Maud Saul Shotton Co Durham
DIED 19TH March 1944
DONALD GILBERT M. BRINE   Portsmouth Memorial
AB P/JX 312434 age 22   Panel 81 Col 2
son of Robert B. & Kate Brine Southwick Wilts   President III
DIED 19th March 1944

KENNETH COOKE
AB D/JX 444481 age 19
son of Thomas & Elizabeth Anne Cook of
High Openshaw Manchester
DIED 19th MARCH 1944

Plymouth Memorial
Panel 86 Col 1
President III

JACK STEEL HOPE
AB D/JX 550918 age 20
DIED 9th MARCH 1944**

Plymouth Memorial
Panel 86 Col 3
President III

** Jack Steel Hope: Date of Death given by General Register of Shipping &
Seaman, Cardiff is 19th March 1944 Prisoner of War died in Japanese
hands. Commonwealth War Graves listing gives 9th March 1944. However
in an unsworn statement made by Mr. W. Phillips, Chief Officer of the
"BEHAR" who survived captivity, Jack Steel Hope was last seen aboard the
Japanese cruiser "TONE" on 16th March 1944 at Tandjong Priok, along with
other prisoners who were ultimately killed on the night of 18/19th March
1944 after ship sailed Tandjong Priok.

Naval Asdic Personnel
ROBERT IDRIS WILLIAMS
A/B D/SSX 35901 age 22
son of Morris & Jane Williams of Dyffryn
Merrionethshire
DIED 19TH MARCH 1944

Plymouth Memorial
Panel 87 Col 3
President III

STANLEY ENOCH
AB D/JX 393587 age 20
Son of Stanley & Dorothy M Enoch of Caerau Maesteg
Glamorgan
DIED 19th MARCH 1944

Plymouth Memorial
Panel 101 Col 2
President III

Army personnel
4th Maritime Regiment Royal Artillery

ARTHUR BOWERS
Bdr 6290844 age 23
DIED 18/19th MARCH 1944
ALFRED STREET
Gnr 11259712 age 34
DIED 18/19th MARCH 1944
1st Maritime Regiment Royal Artillery

Plymouth Memorial
Panel 93 Col 2

Plymouth Memorial
Panel 93 Col 2

CHARLIE RATCLIFFE   Portsmouth Memorial
SGT 3441983 age 37   Panel 88 Col 2
son of Ernest & Elizabeth Ratcliffe. Husband of
Nancy Ratcliffe of Hollinwood Lancs
DIED 18/19th MARCH 1944

ALEX RODNEY   Portsmouth Memorial
Gnr 1656736 age 37   Panel 88 Col 2
son of Joseph & Bethia Rodney of Greenock
DIED 18/19th MARCH 1944

NEIL BRODIE   Portsmouth Memorial
Bdr 3326794 age 33   Panel 88 Col 2
son of Neil & Jessie Brown Brodie. Husband of
Margaret R. Brodie of Campbletown Argyllshire
DIED 18/19th MARCH 1944

Passenger
DUNCAN MacGREGOR
British citizen retired bank manager from Kenya. Residing in
Burwood, Victoria, Australia en route from Australia to Kenya
via Bombay.

Indian crew

Name	Age	Number	Rank
MAHOMED ABBA	50	82887	Tindel
NALLA ESMAIL	34	17130	Seacunny
HOOSEIN ESMAIL	31	12263	Seacunny
BEELAL DAWOODJEE	31	21921	Lascar
MOOSSA YACOOB	45	4/3406	Lascar
GOOLAB CASSAM	30	10083	Lascar
HOOSEIN PEERAN	37	2/4038	Lascar
EUSOOF MANJEE	43	3187	Lascar
ADAM ABAJEE	55	77299	Lascar
DAWOOD AHMED	49	84659	Lascar
JEEWA AHMED	29	22202	Lascar
DAWOOD TAJA	40	3/367	Lascar
ADAM DAWOOD	57	61641	Lascar
SULLEYMAN AMONJEE	26	23467	Lascar
CASSAM MAHOMED	27	22796	Lascar
HAJI ADAM	36	42235	Lascar
DAWOOD CASSAM	36	42237	Lascar
BELAL MAHOMED	21	32124	Lascar

MAHOMED AMONJEE	20	42236 Lascar Boy
BABOO RAMJAM	43	4/2005 Bhandary
MAHOMED KHAN GOOLAB	53	99553 1st Paniwalla
ZARIF KHAN KHOOSHAL	58	62998 1st Paniwalla
BARAM GOOL AKMAD	49	3/3399 1st Paniwalla
MAHOMED AMZULLA	45	01150 2nd Paniwalla
HOOSEIN KHAN KHAIRULLA KHAN	43	3/9359 3rd Paniwalla
MIRZADA KHOSHAL	23	28986 Tindel
NABIULLA AMIRULLA	31	422234 Fireman
HAZARATDEEN OOMERDEEN	51	96509 Engine Bhandary

Goanese crew

SANTAN VIEGAS	45	89662 Chief Cook
JOHN DE SOUZA	28	27734 Baker
JOAQUIM S CONTINHO	57	64687 Pantryman
JOAQUIM X DE SOUZA	53	07006 G.S.
LONSADO DIAS	26	35961 G.S.
NICOLAO VALLES	45	5541 G.S.
GLORIA DIAS	24	26652 G.S.
BENJAMIN ALMEIDA	51	55056 G.S.
FULARIAN SILVA	23	033224 G.S.
SEBASTIAO VAZ	46	08056 G.S.
VINCENT DENIZ	45	238 Topass
JOAO BARRETTO	45	8395 Topass

Chinese crew

| AH SANG | 30 | Carpenter |
| WONG CHAK | 28 | Fitter |

APPENDIX 3

The following personnel were killed on the "BEHAR" during the shelling by the Japanese cruiser "TONE" on 9th March 1944.

DEMS
THOMAS ROBINSON   Chatham Memorial
AB C/JX 248976 age 23   Panel 76 Col 1
                                   President III

4th Maritime Regiment Royal Artillery

STANLEY PYECROFT	Plymouth Memorial
Gnr 11416381 Son of Frank and Lelita	
Pyecroft of Nottingham	Panel 93 Col 2
age 21	

Indian crew	Age	Number	Rating
EMAD NOOR KHAN	55	05967	2ND Paniwalla

APPENDIX 4

The following Indian Crew died in captivity in JAVA.

	Age	Number	Rating
HOSSEIN BEELAL	35	4/4014	DECK SERANG died of dysentery 27.5.44 Del Rosea hospital.
JOOMA KHAN KAMROODEEN	31	34853	FIREMAN died of dysentery 21.5.44 Naval Barracks Batavia.
Goanese			
JOAO SANTAN CONTINHO	63	47900	BUTLER died May 1944. Taken from Naval Barracks, Batavia in dying condition.

The following Chinese passenger, was taken away by the Japanese from the P.O.W. camp in June 1944 and was not seen again.
LAI YUNG LI - Doctor of Agriculture. This passenger had been en route to Chunking University.

APPENDIX 5

SURVIVORS OF CAPTIIVITY
Officers

CAPTAIN M. SYMONS	survived captivity in JAPAN
CHIEF OFFICER W.PHILLIPS	survived captivity in JAVA
CHIEF ENGINEER J.WEIR	survived captivity in JAVA
1st RADIO OFFICER A.C.R. WALKER	survived captivity in JAPAN

Indian Crew
Survivors after captivity in JAVA

	Age	Number	Rating
GAFOOR FACKEER GODAL	23	14433	Seacunny
ESMAIL IBRAHIM	43	38168	Seacunny
CASSAM ESHMAIL	43	4/2778	Seacunny
CASSAM HOOSEIN	33	2/165	Seacunny
KHADY FATHOOLA	53	81892	Fireman Serang
RAZAKHAN SHADAD	45	4/2448	1st Paniwalla
FAZULDAD OOMAR	34	23477	1st Paniwalla
RAZEE KHAN MOOZAD KHAN	35	10092	3rd Paniwalla
GOOL KHAN FAZALDAD	47	4253	Tindel
MAHOMED ALLAM NOORDEEN	43	5	Fireman
GOOLAM SHAN ABDOOLA SHAH	26	38298	Fireman
KARUM KHAN LATIF KHAN	26	32733	Fireman

Goanese

JOHN ROZARIO PEREIRA	26	24525	2nd Cook
JOAO FERNANDES	28	30595	2nd Cook
PHILLIP REBELLO	49	063592	G.S.
DOMINIC P. FERNANDES	46	35274	G.S
MANUEL FERNANDES	34	27504	Topass

DEMS Crew
Gunners
PETTY OFFICER W.L. GRIFFITHS
P/JX 185951   Survived captivity in JAVA

R.N. ASDIC Operators
C.P.H.KERSHAW AB D/JX 187547   Survived captivity in JAVA
A.MacLEOD AB C/JX 240098   Survived captivity in JAVA

Passengers
CAPTAIN P.J. GREEN   Survived captivity in JAPAN
FLT.SGT BARR   Survived captivity in JAVA
LT.S.C. PARKER   Survived captivity in JAPAN
SUB.LT. J.R. BENGE   Survived captivity in JAPAN
SUB.LT. J.G.GODWIN   Survived captivity in JAPAN
MRS A.C. SHAW   Survived captivity in JAVA
MRS G.PASCHEOVE   Survived captivity in JAVA

APPENDIX 6

Composition of soles on board the "BEHAR" taken from records supplied by General Registry of Shipping & Seamen.
Composition of survivors taken from statements made by Chief Officer,

various records at PRO. KEW and General Register of Shipping & Seaman.

 <u>18</u> Officers
 63 Indian ratings including 2 Chinese ratings
 13 DEMS R.N. & Royal Artillery Regiment Gunners
  4 R.N. Asdic Operators
  <u>9</u> Passengers

107 Total
  <u>3</u> Killed in action

<u>104</u> taken prisoner.
 15 European crew and passengers landed
     (4 Officers, 1 Petty Officer (gunner)
     2 asdic operators and 8 passengers including the two females
     and Chinese passenger)
 20 Indians landed

 69 Executed on "TONE"

Breakdown of numbers		
Officers on "BEHAR"	18	
Landed in JAVA	<u>4</u>	
Left on "TONE"	14	Executed 14
Indian Crew on "BEHAR"	61	
Chinese Crew on "BEHAR"	<u>2</u>	
	63	
Indian killed on "BEHAR"	1	
	62	
Indians landed in JAVA	<u>20</u>	
Left on "TONE"	42	Executed 42
Passengers on "BEHAR"	9	
Left on "TONE"	1	
	<u>8</u>	Executed 1
DEMS/R.A. Personnel	17	
Killed on "BEHAR"	<u>2</u>	
	15	
Landed in JAVA	<u>3</u>	
Left on "TONE"	12	Executed 12

Executed on "TONE" 27 EUROPEANS 40 INDIANS & 2 CHINESE.
APPENDIX 7

Seperation on the "TONE" in Tandjong Priok of prisoners – details
provided by Chief Officer Mr.W.Phillips after being released from captivity.
18th March 1944 landed ashore and taken to Batavia Naval Barracks

Group 1

Captain Symons
Chief Officer Phillips
Chief Engineer Weir
1st Radio Officer Walker
Petty Officer Griffiths
McLeod Asdic Rating
Kershaw Asdic Rating

Passengers
Captain Green
Dr Lee
Lt Parker
Sub.Lt. Benge
Sub.Lt Godwin
Flt.Sgt Barr
Mrs Pascheove
Mrs Shaw

April 18-28 1944 split up for interrogation by Kem Pei Tei. Solitary confinement.

Group 2

Chief Officer Phillips
Chief Engineer Weir
Sub.Lt. Godwin*
Flt.Sgt Barr
Kershaw
McLeod
Griffiths
Dr Lee

April 28th 1944 Group 2 returned to naval barracks to find 20 of Lascar crew there.

May 21st 1944 Short re-union with Captain Symons etc, before Group 2* handed over to Jap Military, placed in dark cells at P.O.W. No1 Batavia.

*not Godwin
May 22nd 1944
Returned to naval barracks for 2 hours then back again to P.O.W. camp.

May 22nd 1944 women seperated and removed to civil internment camp.
May 22nd 1944 to March 18th 1945 group of 6 kept in isolated imprisonment

114

Chief Officer Phillips
Chief Engineer Weir
Petty Officer Griffiths
Flt Sgt. Barr
A.B. Kershaw
A.B. McLeod

March 18th 1945 Shifted from isolation to main camp.

June 18th 1945 Removed with draft to camp at Bandoeng.

August 24th 1945 Removed back to Batavia.

September 24th 1945 Rescued by R.A.P.W.I.

Prisoners given no POW number until July 1945

Japanese Commanders at Batavia POW camp.
Lt.Maruyama to December 1944
Lt.Karashima to June 1945

Author's note.
Prison camp in Batavia ex barracks of the 10th Battalion of the Dutch Colonial Army, K.N.L.I. – KONINKLIJKE NEDERLANDS-INDIE LEGER. The 10th was a bicycle unit. The prioners called the place "BICYCLE CAMP"

APPENDIX 8

Prisoners transferred to Japan, sailing June or July 1944 from Sourabaya Java in Japanese ship SANUKI MARU to Osaka via Singapore.

Captain Symons
Captain Green
1st Radio Officer Walker
Lt. Parker
Sub.Lt Godwin
Sub.Lt. Benge

Radio Officer Walker signed sworn affidavit concerning ill treatment on voyage to Japan.
WO 311/562 file PRO KEW

Captain Green taken to Ofuna interrogation camp and later to
Imori P.O.W. camp

APPENDIX 9

DEMS EQUIPMENT

4 inch and 3 inch dual prupose guns.
Oerlikon guns, Browning machine guns, rocket launcher.
Anti-submarine detection equipment (ASDIC)

Information supplied by Petty Officer Walter L. Griffiths
I/C Dems party "BEHAR"

Voyage of M.S. BEHAR after completeion by shipbuilders August 1943.

Arrived	Sailed
Clyde anchorage 20/8	21/8
Liverpool 22/8	11/9
Clyde anchorage 12/9	15/9
Suez 29/9	29/9
Aden 3/10	9/10
Cochin 16/10	27/10
Bombay 30/10	7/11
Karachi 9/11	18/11
Ceylon 22/11	23/11
Calcutta in port 27/28 November	
1944	
Ceylon 1/1/44	9/1
Fremantle 18/1	20/1
Adelaide 24/1	26/1
Melbourne 28/1	3/2
Wellington 7/2	
Sydney 16/2	
Newcastle N.S.W.	22/2
Melbourne 25/2	29/2

Information from Guild Hall Library London "Lloyd's Shipping Collection"

APPENDIX 10

Letter from Hain Steamship Company to Judge Advocate General's Office

Source PRO KEW WO 311/564

THE HAIN STEAMSHIP COMPANY LIMITED

Baltic Exchange Chambers,
St.Mary Axe, London E.C. 3

8th March 1947

MD/JAG/FS/JM/23 (2G)

CONFIDENTIAL

Judge Advocate General,
Spring Gardens,
Cockspur Street,
London S.W.1

Dear Sir,

Japanese War Crimes. Sinking of m.v. "BEHAR" and Alleged Massacre of 69 Survivors thereof.

We are in receipt of your letter of the 6th instant, and note you are endeavouring to discover the fate of Gordon Henry Cumming, who was listed as 3rd Radio Officer on board the above named vessel when she was sunk by the Japanese cruiser "TONI" in the Indian Ocean on the 9th March, 1944.

In reply to your enquiry, we have to advise you that the Director General, Ministry of War Transport, Berkeley Square House, London S.W.1., writing to us on the 13th April 1946 under reference M.14553/45, advised that it had then been established that the survivors of the M.V. "BEHAR", who were taken aboard the Japanese cruiser which sank the vessel and who were not subsequently landed in Batavia, were executed on the cruiser on the night of the 18/19th March, 1944.

We were requested that this information should be communicated to the next of kin with an expression of the Minister's deepest sympathy. At the same time we were asked to inform the relatives that the Minister greatly regretted the delay in communicating this information, which was necessary to ensure the apprehension of the person responsible for this appalling crime.

Captain M.G. Symons, who was Master of the "BEHAR" at the time of her loss, is now Master of our M.V. "TREVOSE", which vessel is now at St.John, N.B. Chief Officer W. Phillips is also in the "TREVOSE". Chief Engineer J. McKay Weir and 1st Radio Officer A.C.R. WALKER are no longer in our employ, and in the case of the former we suggest you communicate with him at his home address, 140, Lochleven Road,

117

Langside, Glasgow. The latter is resident at 8, Carlyle Avenue, Southall, Middx. We would add that Messrs. Symons, Phillips, Weir and Walker were originally landed at Batavia, and in consequence they would have no first-hand knowledge of the massacre of the 69 survivors who were retained on the Japanese cruiser, and we therefore suggest you obtain the required confirmation from the Director General, Ministry of Transport, London, S.W.1.

Yours faithfully,
For THE HAIN STEAMSHIP COMPANY, LIMITED,

(Signed) J.Roach,
Asst. Secretary.

Author's note.
Note the incorrect spelling of the cruiser's name.

Considerable correspondence exists in the files from Mr. H.G. Cumming to the Judge Advocate General's office, and other authorities trying to find out what had happened to his son who had joined the BEHAR at Calcutta on 3rd November 1943, replacing the previous 3rd Radio Officer, and had failed to come home after the war ended.